WALKING
BESIDE
ME

MARICOR GO-BROZO

An Imprint for GracePoint Publishing (www.GracePointPublishing.com)

GracePoint Matrix, LLC
322 N Tejon St. #207
Colorado Springs CO 80903
www.GracePointMatrix.com
Email: Admin@GracePointMatrix.com
SAN # 991-6032

Library of Congress Control Number: 2020950289

ISBN-13: (Paperback) 978-1-951694-27-2
eISBN (eBook) 978-1-951694-28-9

Books may be purchased for educational, business, or sales promotional use.
For bulk order requests and price schedule contact:
Orders@GracePointPublishing.com

Printed in the United States of America
Additional books printed and published by the author with permission from publisher.

"When God is doing something great, and you are in the midst of it, be grateful."

Anonymous

TABLE OF CONTENTS

FOREWORD

Dear Reader,

We are all on a journey in life — roads with twists and turns that take us in many directions leading us forward to our destination. You may find yourself, today, on a pathway of peace, or perhaps one of uncertainty as to what is around the next bend or even at a crossroads wondering . . . which way should I go?

I met Marshi on one leg of her journey and have walked alongside her through the pages you hold in your hand. You may say to yourself — In my busy life, there are so many books, and so little time, why this book? Why now?

This book is for you, for such a time as now. As you delve into the impactful words on these pages, you may discover answers for today or in preparation for tomorrow. May I invite you to join me and experience one woman's incredible journey one step at a time?

"You see, before leaving the Netherlands, I had completed an Excel spreadsheet showing the schedule of each member of the family for the whole six weeks. I had written where each one of us would be on a particular day and at a specific time. It was all set. And everything had gone exactly as planned, until this week."

Marshi finds herself on an unexpected path; and as you walk with her, you will explore steps in your own path bringing a deeper understanding to your own personal journey. You will be encouraged, empowered, and inspired by this amazing woman of courage and faith.

As you move through each day, take time to pause and ponder the nuggets of wisdom and truths she shares along the way. You will be changed as I was and be ever grateful to have traveled this road.

Not only does she take you into the deepest part of her heart, but she also becomes your companion and friend through her transparency as she shares the most intimate thoughts of her soul.

"This had become our journey together, not only mine, not only of the family."

Time spent in *Walking Beside Me* has not only challenged and inspired me on my own journey, but I have also come away embracing each new day, whatever it holds, with courage, zeal, and anticipation, looking forward to the future with joy.

And, I have made a treasured friend along the way.

Looking forward,

Tita Laurie
California, September 2020

PREFACE

The world is almost at a standstill because of the pandemic caused by the novel coronavirus. Lives have been lost, businesses closed, jobs prematurely terminated, and plans and dreams put on hold. It's like we are all having a nightmare and we can't wait to wake up!

Only two months into the government-imposed lockdown in Metro Manila, where the capital city of the Philippines sits, friends and their loved ones have succumbed to COVID-19. Some were put on life support before they eventually passed away. I learned about their experiences, and they were remarkably similar to what I went through in 2019. I wished I had written a book about my experience so that others could have learned from it and perhaps be comforted knowing that someone had already gone through the same journey. But I wasn't ready to revisit the most painful experience our family has ever gone through. Ever since my husband died, my focus has been to move forward with my kids. I had not looked back since then; not in a way that I would intentionally recall the details of the events that happened during Ryan's last twenty-five days.

August 13, 2020, a year after the day we took Ryan to the hospital with a sudden illness, I began recalling the details of the twenty-five-day journey of his departure. More than anything else, I intended it to help me in my own healing process. As I posted my daily entries on my Facebook account, I received numerous messages from friends and former colleagues whom I haven't talked to or seen for years, telling me how my experience has comforted, encouraged, and inspired them in their own journeys in life. They patiently (and at times quietly) followed the story, one day at a time even when they already knew the ending. Many even said it was like watching a TV series; they had to wait for the next post for the continuation of the story. Others said if it were a book, they would want to hold the pages in their hands and read them all over again.

It dawned on me that we all have our own struggles in varying degrees. Some may have health problems, others financial problems, and some relational problems. It is when life isn't going well for us that the manner by which we try to survive each day and face tomorrow becomes impactful to the people around us — those who have gone through hardships, those who are going through problems, and those who are bound to face challenges in their lives.

Walking Beside Me is the product of my desire to share a story of God's trustworthiness, even when everything in life tells you otherwise. My faith in His sovereignty has given me peace amidst the most heartbreaking experience in my life. I hope this book will reach many, and that many lives will be inspired to keep on and to hold on to the One who is in control of what lies beyond today.

The Author

My dearest Samantha and Shaun,

It has been a year since your dad went to heaven. You were just nine years old, Sam, while you, Shaun, were two. Everything happened unexpectedly. While visiting our family in Manila for the first time since we moved to Amsterdam in 2018, your dad got sick. We haven't left the Philippines since then.

I am recounting your dad's final twenty-five days for you. At the right time, you will read this book and understand that amid great trials, we can have perfect peace because Christ is enough for us.

I love you both so dearly, just as much as your dad loved you: with all his heart.

With all my love,
Mommy

INTRODUCTION

After a three-kilometer run at midday, Ryan and I found ourselves enjoying a nice walk along the canals just at the back of our house. It was a beautiful, cool, and sunny day, perfect Amsterdam weather, I would say.

"Mommy," Ryan said to me (we had started calling each other "Mommy" and "Dad" nine years ago when our daughter, Samantha, was born), "I look forward to retiring here in the Netherlands with you. I can imagine us enjoying long walks or cycling together when we are old."

"Yes, Dad," I replied. "I would love that. And maybe we could just sit at the park while we read a book."

We held hands as we walked back to the house. It was just 1:00 p.m. We worked from home that day and had just spent our lunch break on a short run. This was one of the many things we both loved about the Netherlands. We could run at any time of the day because the weather permitted us to do so.

We grabbed brewed coffee and some homemade sandwiches and continued our work in our own corner of the dining table. Ryan had two hours before it was time for him to fetch our kids

— Samantha at school, and Shaun, after another two hours, at his daycare. Sam was nine years old, while Shaun was two.

Before I knew it, Ryan had already fetched Sam. And as always, the first thing Sam wanted was a sandwich. Yes, we were a Filipino family who lived on pancakes, sandwiches, and pasta, and could survive without rice for weeks. Sam prepared her ever favorite Nutella sandwich and joined us at the dining table for a chat.

It was only three days before the end of the school year and three days before our flight to Hong Kong.

As Sam enjoyed her snack, we talked about our plans for our upcoming six-week holiday in Asia — a week in Hong Kong and five weeks in Manila. It was not exactly five weeks of holiday in Manila because Ryan and I would be working remotely for two weeks. We were all so excited about our first "homecoming." All bags had been packed, and we were ready to go. Well, we were not quite ready, but extremely excited.

At 5:30, Ryan got Shaun from his daycare while I started to prepare dinner. Sam went to Sara's house to play for a while. Sara was one of her best friends in school. Dinner was ready by the time the three Brozos arrived.

"I want to go to the beach!" exclaimed the little one. Even Shaun had his own plan.

*****

Five weeks later, August 11, 2019, we had our last outing with family and friends in Laguna, a province in the southern part of the Philippines. That was the last weekend before we would head back to the Netherlands. We rented a private pool resort, and

Sam and Shaun enjoyed every moment swimming with their dad. Shaun wore a swimming vest but spent most of the time clinging on to Ryan because he was scared to float on his own. At one point, Shaun didn't realize that Ryan had let go of him and he was floating without support from his dad. After Shaun found his new courage to float and swim on his own, he didn't want to be assisted anymore and was, in fact, the last person to get out of the pool.

It was a beautiful time with family and friends. It was a moment I wish I could relive. It was a special memory I will cherish in my heart forever.

PART I

INTO THE UNKNOWN

Ryan and I went to Parañaque Doctors' Hospital (PDH) that morning to have his laboratory test taken and to see a doctor. He had been suffering from a high fever and severe headache for three days. The doctor advised Ryan to be admitted for close monitoring. There was, however, no available room, so we went back home and decided that my sister Naty, who is a doctor, would monitor him. We turned our living room into a makeshift hospital room and put an IV into Ryan to ensure he was kept hydrated. There was nothing more we could do at the time but to monitor him and wait for the result of the laboratory test and for an available room at PDH.

We brought Ryan back to PDH that evening for an electroencephalogram (EEG) and cranial computed tomography (CT) scan to determine what was causing his severe headache. A room had become available and Ryan was admitted to the hospital.

This was our first night in the hospital.

We didn't talk much because he was in severe pain. I just made sure I attended to his needs. When he fell asleep, I took that time to step back and assess what was happening and what could possibly happen.

In the silence of the moment, my mind became filled with so many thoughts. I entertained the possibility of losing Ryan. I tried to think of what I would do if that happened. What would life be like for the kids without him? Ryan was their playmate, music teacher, computer guru, art buddy, companion in all their adventurous activities, and the in-house, self-anointed "doctor." I had always said that I couldn't be to the kids what Ryan was to them. I wasn't sure I knew how to move forward. That couldn't be one of the possibilities. It just couldn't.

I had to cast off those negative thoughts and sent prayer requests to friends and families in my different group chats. It would have been easier to post a message on my Facebook wall, however, many of our friends didn't know we were in the Philippines on holiday, so I patiently texted various groups with updates and prayer requests.

Ryan's EEG and CT scan results were normal. With several concerns of what Ryan could be suffering from, we were now able to remove aneurysm from the list. His x-ray result, however, showed he had pneumonia, and additional tests still had to be done to rule out dengue. It was the rainy season in Manila when dengue was at its peak.

Ryan and I talked that day. I asked him how he felt about what was happening. He was disappointed. This was not part of our six-week holiday plan. You see, before leaving the Netherlands, I had completed an Excel spreadsheet showing the schedule of each member of the family for the whole six weeks. I had written where each one of us would be on a particular day and at a specific time. It was all set. And everything had gone exactly as planned, until this week. This was the final week of our holiday in Manila and, naturally, we wanted to spend our remaining days with family. I understood how Ryan felt. We didn't want to spend our final week at the hospital.

Sam and Shaun, with their cousins, went to see their dad at PDH. This turned out to be the kids' last visit with Ryan. After we were told Ryan had pneumonia, we didn't allow the kids to see their dad while he was in the hospital. This was the last time the kids saw Ryan awake, their last time to hear his voice. It was also Ryan's last time to hear the kids' laughter and playful noise. There were no more hugs and kisses.

Later that evening, I asked Cris, my youngest sister, to stay with Ryan while I bought some items at a nearby drugstore. I was accompanied by my dear friend, Charo, who also visited that day. As we walked toward the drugstore, I asked Charo if we could stop by the parking lot and go inside her car. I just cried and poured everything out. I told her I wouldn't know what to do if Ryan died. God couldn't take him away yet. From that time on, I prayed for healing and good health, and chose to believe that God would heal Ryan and restore his health. That was the only way I could go through this.

Ryan had fallen ill in the past, but it wasn't serious enough for him to be admitted to a hospital. This was, in fact, the first time Ryan was hospitalized during our marriage. At the time, there was no indication he was gravely ill. Why did I think Ryan would die, that I would lose Ryan, when the diagnosis at the time was only pneumonia? I cannot give an answer. I think I just wanted to cover all possibilities, both good and bad, and that was one direction I knew I didn't want to take.

When I went back to the hospital room, my eyes were swollen. Surely, Ryan noticed I'd been crying, but he didn't say anything. He just allowed me to catch up on my sleep that evening.

Ryan was an exceptionally good patient; he made no complaints, which was very uncharacteristic of him. Whenever he was sick, he would agonize as though it were the end of the world. I guess some wives could relate to this when their husbands exaggerate. I loved Ryan for his imperfection, but he was different this time. He was sick but remarkably silent.

Lo and behold! When I woke up, Ryan had already showered, changed clothes, and shaved. I asked him why he didn't wake me up. He replied that he wanted me to get more sleep because he knew I was exhausted. His love and selflessness, even when feeling unwell, touched my heart.

Later that morning, we did a video call with the kids to check on them and just chat. The family missed being together, especially our little boy.

As the attending doctor had not yet ruled out dengue, Ryan's blood platelet count was monitored daily. It was steadily going down since he had his blood sample taken. From 182 four days earlier, it was down to 110. The normal platelet count range for a healthy adult is from 150 to 400. He was also still running a fever.

Ryan and I had another talk that day. We constantly had family and friends visiting, so whenever we were alone and he could talk, I would engage him in a conversation. He shared that he felt bad about the whole situation and asked God why He allowed him to get sick. This was not an unexpected response from Ryan, and I fully understood him. I assured him this would soon be over, and we'd be back in Amsterdam in no time, back to our quiet but happy lives.

Before we arrived in Manila for our holiday, we spent a week in Hong Kong, where my best friend Kaye was based. Our flight back to Amsterdam would also leave from Hong Kong. We were scheduled to fly out of Manila on August 22 to Hong Kong, where we would stay with Kaye for three days, and fly out of Hong Kong to Amsterdam on August 24.

Ryan suggested we pray for what was best. He said that maybe it was an option for the kids and me to go back as scheduled and he would just follow. My heart did not approve of that idea. I told him perhaps we could all fly together on August 24 from Manila to Hong Kong and then take the Hong Kong – Amsterdam flight that we had originally booked. This plan assumed Ryan would become well and be discharged in four days. The doctor then told us that we had to push our flight back by another week.

Later in the evening, the infectious disease doctor saw Ryan and updated us that in addition to pneumonia, Ryan had a systemic viral infection. It was still early to say whether or not he had dengue.

Overall, Ryan was better on this day than the previous days. While he still had a high-grade fever, the doctor expected it would go down starting the next day. His latest platelet count remained at 110 and his headache had also become more tolerable. Ryan was even in good spirits when friends visited him. All this, I thought, was a good indication that Ryan's health condition was "under control."

I had been regularly updating Pinky, Ryan's older and only sibling. Pinky went to a seminary school and after graduating, worked at our church in Tacloban, Leyte as music director. Leyte is an island province in the Visayas group of islands in the Philippines. She married a local pastor, with whom she has two wonderful teenage boys. They are now shepherding a church in Cebu, a province in the Central Visayas region. It was through Pinky that I met Ryan. We were paired as candle bearers in their wedding in Tacloban. As part of God's plan, Pinky played "matchmaker" and introduced Ryan, a city boy, to me, a shy provincial girl. And the rest is history.

Pinky assured me that their church congregation was praying for Ryan. In Amsterdam, our Grace Church family had organized a church-wide prayer for Ryan.

That night, on that small bedside sofa, I rested in Jesus.

Upon the doctor's orders, an oxygen tank was placed on standby in the room. Ryan's oxygen level was already below normal, though he said he had no difficulty breathing.

I requested my brother-in-law Joel to stay with Ryan while Charo and I brought the kids back to the dentist. Ryan really wanted to preserve Shaun's front teeth and during their first visit, the dentist suggested for Shaun to use crowns to prevent further decay. We took a photo of Shaun's front teeth and sent it to their dad.

When I got back to the hospital, Joel and Naty said that Ryan had been talking in his sleep, as though he was experiencing delirium. I also witnessed that many times in the past few days. It came to a point that it terrified me; so, whenever he talked in his sleep, I would wake him up. They said it must have been caused by the high-grade fever.

Ryan's health condition worsened again. His platelet count went down from 110 to 100, and his fever ranged between 38 and 40 degrees Celsius, or between 100.4 and 104 degrees Fahrenheit. His oxygen saturation level, or O_2SAT, was 90 percent, when the normal level is between 95 and 100 percent. His pneumonia had also progressed.

Some time that evening, we noticed Ryan was having labored breathing. When Ryan and I were left alone in the room, I asked him if he wanted to put on an oxygen mask to support his breathing. He asked how much it would cost if he used the oxygen tank. My heart broke when he asked that. I wanted to cry in front of him. He must have been having a hard time already but was thinking of saving on hospital costs. I told him not to worry about anything, especially the financial aspect. We just needed him to get well soon.

After he had put on the oxygen mask, he asked me to take a photo of him and send it to Sam because he looked like Antman, one of our favorite characters in the Avengers universe.

That night, we also admitted our father to PDH. Papa, based in Butuan, Mindanao, visited us during our holiday in Manila. He had been having issues in his abdominal area, so we took the opportunity for him to undergo medical tests and procedures that required his admission to the hospital. We now had two patients in the family.

My heart was heavy. Ryan's condition wasn't improving. In fact, it was worsening rather quickly. I missed the kids, too. I continued to update family and friends through various group chats and asked for prayers.

Later that night, Kaye arrived from Hong Kong. She wasn't supposed to come home to the Philippines this weekend because we were originally scheduled to fly back to Hong Kong the following week; however, because of the unexpected turn of events, she decided to come home. I was so happy to have someone with me in the hospital to take care of Ryan.

Showing our smiles for daddy after our dental check-up.

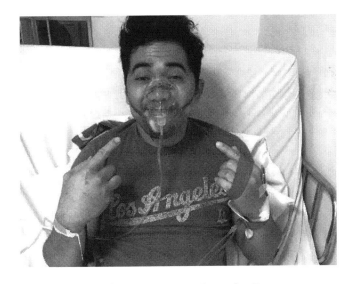

This photo was sent to Sam after Ryan
put on the oxygen mask.

A new doctor was brought on board, a pulmonologist. She saw Ryan and, like a professor, educated us about the lungs. She showed us how healthy lungs looked compared to lungs with pneumonia. It was instructive and we had a better appreciation of the state of Ryan's lungs.

Ryan had pneumonia in the right lung only, but it had progressed dramatically in two days. Ryan was forty years old, athletic, and a non-smoker. With his profile, Ryan's pneumonia was unlikely to progress to the point of requiring high oxygen concentration and strong antibiotics. Tuberculosis (TB) was also a possibility and tests had been done to determine if Ryan had it. In any case, Ryan's immune system was compromised, and the doctor could give no explanation considering his profile.

What comforted me was pneumonia and TB were treatable. The pulmonologist said we had to wait for the test results and the medicines to take effect. Waiting is healing, as the pulmonologist repeatedly said. She wanted Ryan to be transferred to the intensive care unit (ICU) of the hospital so he could be closely monitored. We began to make the arrangements so Ryan could be transferred within the day.

Meanwhile, some good news — dengue had been ruled out, and with Ryan in the ICU, more manpower could be dedicated to Papa and the kids at home. We had been staying at our house on Lebanon Street, which was just a few minutes away from PDH. It was such a blessing that we were surrounded by family; therefore, leaving Sam and Shaun at home with their cousins was not so difficult.

With this development, flying back to Amsterdam was out of the picture. Ryan had been healthy a week earlier. We were scheduled to go back home in another week's time. I had to pause and remind myself about one truth. "God is our refuge and strength, an ever-present help in trouble. Therefore, we will not fear, though the earth gives way and the mountains fall into the heart of the sea." (Psalm 46:1-2 New International Version)

*****

This was a long and eventful day for me.

The infectious disease doctor arrived and asked to speak to Ryan alone. Kaye and I quietly stepped out of the room and waited outside Papa's room, which was also on the same hospital floor.

It puzzled me why the doctor would ask me to go out. At that moment, my heart was beating fast. I told Kaye there was only one reason I could think of why the doctor asked us to leave. The doctor must have been entertaining the possibility that Ryan had HIV and wanted to ask Ryan questions about any extra-marital affairs he may have had. I wouldn't have entertained such a thought in a million years.

After what seemed forever, the doctor came out of the room. Kaye stayed outside so I could talk to Ryan privately. I went inside and tried hard to put on an expressionless face. I sat down on his bed and asked, "Dad, what did you talk about? Why did I have to go out of the room?" I should have received an award for best actress at that moment! Ryan replied in a serious and low voice,

"Mommy, I will tell this to you only." I felt like he just confirmed what I had just told Kaye. I felt like my heart stopped beating. I answered reluctantly, "Ok."

I knew I wasn't prepared for what he was about to say. Ryan said, "The doctor asked me if I had any contact with other women." I was still wearing my deadpan face. He continued, "I told him I have had no sex apart from my wife." At that instant, I felt like all the blood came rushing back to my veins, my heart was beating again. I was ashamed of myself that I entertained the possibility of Ryan being unfaithful to me. I should have known him better. As a next step, Ryan would be tested to determine if he were HIV positive. I understood it. No stone must be left unturned. He was immunocompromised and the doctors wanted to know the cause.

A few minutes later, the family arrived: Naty and her husband, Joel; Cris and her husband, Paolo. Jhaque, our family friend from Leyte who had arrived earlier to provide support, was also with them. Jhaque, a nurse, was surprised to see Ryan struggling with his breathing. Ryan's O2SAT was only 84 percent.

Before he was taken to the ICU, Ryan and I had another private time together. We talked about the things we needed to do: inform his boss in Amsterdam, call the kids' school and daycare, and our insurance company in the Netherlands, among other things. We also needed to transfer our savings from his euro account to my peso account. Ryan and I maintained separate bank accounts in Amsterdam. We put our savings in his bank account and our budget for our daily expenses in my account. To pay for our hospital bill and other expenses, I needed Ryan to transfer some money from his euro account to my peso account that I maintained even after we had moved to Amsterdam. I stopped myself from asking for his PIN code. Why should I ask for the PIN code if he was going to get well? I didn't want to send a wrong signal by asking for passwords and PIN codes. If it meant having a hard time retrieving the PIN codes later, so be it. He did not need any further anxiety. I wished I had asked for his PIN codes and passwords in the same way that I had given him mine. But I wouldn't remember them in any case; I had so many to remember already.

We sang worship songs and he pretended to play the guitar. Ryan was talented in music. He taught himself to play the violin, piano, and guitar. He was part of the music ministry at the congregation we attended both in the Philippines and Netherlands. I asked him to do two things: to PRAY and FIGHT. "You're a fighter, right, Dad?" I asked. "I am a fighter!" he replied.

At around 9:00 p.m., he was taken to the ICU. I gave him one last hug and said, "I love you." I reminded him to pray and fight. It turned out to be my last hug to a conscious Ryan.

After about two hours, we were told Ryan could not breathe on his own and needed to be intubated and attached to a ventilator. Why was this happening so fast? I thanked God I wasn't alone when all of this was happening. I thanked God that He was with me and for providing loved ones in the flesh to be with me at that moment.

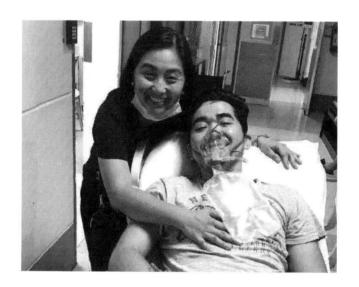

My photo with Ryan right before he
was taken to the ICU of PDH.

The nurses had to sedate Ryan. He had been wrestling with the ICU staff who were struggling to put a breathing tube through his mouth and into his airway. At past midnight, Ryan was finally intubated and attached to a ventilator.

As soon as Ryan woke up from sedation, my sisters Naty and Cris went to check on him while I waited outside the ICU. The only time I saw someone intubated was when Cris had complications after giving birth. I fainted at the sight. I was not prepared to see Ryan this way.

After a few minutes, Naty came out. She told me that the nurses had tied his hands to the bed railings because he was too strong and had tried to pull the tube out of his mouth. Naty said that he looked disoriented and confused, but that she was able to calm him down by telling him that the restraints would be removed if he stopped struggling.

Naty also told me that she had given him paper and a pen so he could communicate. She showed me the first thing he had written.

"Go home to my comfort zone."

When asked where home was, he had written, "Lebanon, with Mama."

He was referring to his mother, Mama Nila; while Lebanon was the street on which our house in Manila was located.

We all went home at around 2:00 a.m. and allowed Ryan to rest. Before I went to bed, I texted Pinky and asked if she had any plans of coming to Manila. I wanted to tell her to come but couldn't directly say it. I strongly felt she had to be in Manila, and it had to be soon.

I woke up to Pinky's messages. She had discussed the trip with her husband, and they agreed that Pinky would fly to Manila the next day, Monday. I updated her that Ryan's illness was progressing rapidly. At that time, Naty told me Ryan could have cancer, or HIV, or TB. If we were to choose among these diseases, we'd rather Ryan had TB because it could be treated.

I decided to spend time with the kids before I went back to the hospital again. Naty had gone ahead to check on Ryan. Naty relayed to me that Ryan had started to relax; and, as promised, the ICU staff untied his hands. However, he had not slept since we left him that morning; so, the ICU staff sedated him, hoping it would improve his O2SAT. It was down in the range of 80s to 70s.

When the nurses said he had already used up so many papers, Naty asked in curiosity if anyone had visited him. The nurses said no one. It turned out Ryan had been conversing with them. Ryan told them we lived in Amsterdam and we just came back for a vacation. He joked that, maybe, his body wasn't used to the viruses and bacteria in Manila anymore.

He also told them he had just moved to a new job in Amsterdam. His new job was a milestone for him since he had worked in only one company in the Philippines and continued working remotely for that company even after we moved to the Netherlands. He had joined the new company barely a month before our family holiday that year.

I arrived in the hospital but was hesitant to go inside the ICU room. I was, in fact, fearful to go inside the ICU. I had to be prompted by my sisters. Of course, I knew I needed to see

Ryan. I could not possibly avoid Ryan while he was intubated. I prayed and went in. "When I am afraid, I put my trust in you." (Psalm 56:3 NIV)

When I saw him, he was calm and looked fresh. The sight of him didn't scare me. I asked him if he had already spent time talking to God. He shook his head. I encouraged him to do so. I knew he felt bad toward God. He had the same reaction in January 2018. At that time, we were having a churchwide prayer and fasting, and one of Ryan's prayers was to learn to fully trust in God. Ryan did not expect God to answer his prayer through Sam getting sick. Sam was diagnosed with a kidney disease two months before we were scheduled to leave for the Netherlands. At first, Ryan did not take it very well and felt bad toward God. After Ryan and I processed the situation and realized this was God's way of answering his prayer, Ryan fully surrendered Sam's health to God. In September 2018, when Sam was seen by a specialist in Amsterdam, she was cleared of her kidney problem. The doctor said Sam's kidneys were 100% good. It was amazing. Indeed, God allowed Ryan to learn to completely trust in Him through that experience. This time, with his illness, I encouraged him to spend time in prayer.

Ryan was uneasy. He asked for his cellphone. I knew what he would do with it, research his illness, and I didn't want to give it to him. I asked why he wanted it. He pointed to his wrist as if to say he wanted to check the time. If it was the time that he wanted to know, I suggested that we put a clock in the room. He reluctantly agreed.

He then asked for a thermometer. He wanted to monitor his fever. I reminded him why he was transferred to the ICU — for the doctors and nurses to monitor him round the clock. I told him to just allow the nurses to do their job. He kept looking at the monitor to see his O2SAT, heart rate, and blood pressure. I was not sure if that was helping him. We asked the nurses to turn the monitor around so he wouldn't see it. Knowing Ryan, he wanted to know what was happening. We didn't call him pseudo-Dr. Brozo for nothing.

The pulmonologist came to check on him. Before she left, she asked Ryan, "Do you have any questions?" Ryan wrote, "Are things going ok? What's the prognosis?" The doctor looked at me and asked, "Should I answer him?" I replied, "Yes, doctor, please tell him everything. He wants to know what is happening." The doctor told us that his situation was not improving; on the contrary, it was getting worse, fast. She told Ryan he needed to rest. We all left after that. The doctor commented that Ryan was an intelligent patient and asked good questions.

That day, family and friends came over to visit Ryan and Papa. When Ryan's cousins visited him, he wrote, "Will Pinky still see me alive?" What was Ryan thinking? After they stepped out of the ICU, one cousin immediately called Pinky and strongly encouraged her to come to Manila that day and not to wait until Monday anymore.

Sam came to the hospital to visit her dad. I took her to the ICU and the two of us stood for a moment just outside Ryan's room. Ryan was asleep, a tube in his mouth and several lines running from his arms to different monitors.

I asked Sam if she wanted to go inside the room to see her dad up close. She said no. Instead, she asked me what all the numbers on the monitor meant. When I explained to her that we were monitoring her dad's oxygen level, she asked what the critical level was. How just like her dad she was!

I told her it was already at critical level and she should pray hard for her dad to get well. I could see that she was fighting back tears, and my heart went out to her – my nine-year old girl who has always been emotionally strong.

*****

I discussed with my family whether we needed to transfer Ryan to another hospital. I prayed earnestly for wisdom to make the right decisions.

At past 10:00 p.m., Pinky arrived from Cebu. She had taken an earlier flight. I was happy and relieved to see her. I needed Pinky to be with me in this tough time. We waited for Ryan to be awake to surprise him.

At midnight, I knocked on the ICU door and asked if Pinky could see Ryan. The nurse was gracious enough to let her in. A few minutes later, the nurse came out of the ICU. "The patient is asking for his wife." I got up and slowly walked toward the door. "He wants everyone to go inside," added the nurse. I wondered in my mind why he wanted to see everyone. I thought, is this goodbye? I, together with family members present at the time, went inside, and joined Pinky.

Ryan had just been given a bath, and he looked refreshed, awake, and alert. He scribbled on a paper, "Why are you here early?" I answered, "Of course, we're excited to see you because you just took a bath." He gave us a smile.

At 9:00 a.m., Naty visited Ryan. He was awake.

Naty asked, "Rye, your O$_2$SAT is not improving when you're awake. Why aren't you sleeping?"

Ryan wrote, "Because this doesn't seem like an isolation room. It's noisier here than in the private room."

Naty then turned to the nurse, "Nurse, look at what the patient wrote."

The nurse replied, "If we close the door, we won't be able to see him."

Ryan wrote, "There should be a buzzer!"

"We have a buzzer, but it is broken," the nurse responded.

The nurse then moved her table to the room entrance, such that even if the door were closed, she could see Ryan.

Pinky came in next. She talked to Ryan about his feelings toward God and encouraged him to submit to God's plan. Pinky and their relatives were entertaining the thought that God was calling Ryan to the ministry, and that God was telling him to fully surrender. Pinky sang to Ryan to comfort him, and he applauded and gave her a thumbs up.

Ryan had to be sedated again to put him to sleep and prevent his O2SAT from going down. Before the nurses sedated Ryan, I went to see him. He simply said, "I have nothing to say, Mommy." I touched his legs and said, "It's okay, Dad, you need to rest now. No need to say anything." This turned out to be my last conversation with him. Looking back now, it pains me so much that I was unable to tell him many things about us, the kids, the future. How could that have been our last conversation?

Charo had suggested we consider transferring Ryan to Makati Medical Center, a tertiary hospital located in the country's central business district, where their family pulmonologist is an active consultant. I relayed this suggestion to Naty, but I had not personally decided to do so.

While Naty was at the operating room, where Papa had been taken for his scheduled medical procedures, she provided the pulmonologist at Makati Med with the summary of Ryan's case, including all the tests and treatment done. Naty also asked Ryan's pulmonologist at PDH if she would recommend transferring him to another hospital. The Makati Med doctor had initially told Naty that it seemed Ryan's doctors at PDH had done everything they could, and she could not guarantee they could do more at Makati Med.

I had to make the decision. A difficult decision. Of course, I wanted to give the best health care to Ryan. I had a lot of confidence in his doctors at PDH. And if the doctor at Makati Med thought everything had already been done at PDH and she couldn't guarantee they could do more, then why transfer him? I recognized we didn't have the money, but that was not the reason why I wasn't initially convinced.

At the time, I was in Papa's room with Liezl, Cristy, and Jhaque. Papa was still in the recovery room after his procedure. I asked them to give me some time to pray. I lay down on Papa's bed and cried out to God. I asked for a clear sign that we should transfer Ryan. Naty later arrived and told us that the doctor at Makati Med said they had a machine called an ECMO machine (extracorporeal membrane oxygenation), an artificial heart-lung machine that helps deliver oxygen to the body. She said this would give the doctors time to find out what was wrong with Ryan. When I heard that, I knew my prayer had been answered. We decided to transfer him. The coordination between the two hospitals began.

Cris asked me whether I wanted our sister Ann, who was in London, to come home or just send the money instead, to help with the hospital bill. I told Cris that although we needed money, I wanted Ann's presence more than anything. That day at noon, Ann immediately bought a ticket and flew that evening.

When Papa was brought back to his room, I told him about Ryan's condition and that we would be transferring him to Makati Med. Papa comforted me by saying "God is in control of everything that happens in our lives," and for the first time in decades, I cried like a little girl as I lay beside him. I was completely overwhelmed by all that was happening.

Everything that was happening was unexpected, unplanned, unwanted!

At 8:00 p.m., the ambulance from Makati Med arrived at PDH. We had only a thirty-minute window to transfer Ryan. The portable mechanical ventilators used in ambulances do not provide the required settings to sustain Ryan's O2SAT to at least 90 percent. It could be life-threatening if travel time took longer than thirty minutes. Naty and Pinky stayed with Ryan in the ambulance, while I followed them in Kaye's car. We prayed for safety and the rush hour traffic to ease up. Before Kaye drove off, she assured me, "Marshi, I will drive very fast; but don't worry, you will be safe, ok?" Jhaque and Cris would later follow us to Makati Med.

We made it to the Makati Med emergency unit in under thirty minutes. When the ambulance stopped, Ryan unbuckled his seatbelt. He was conscious of what was happening, although that time, his O2SAT was only at 40 percent!

Accompanied by Naty, Ryan was taken to the emergency room (ER). He was restless and extubated himself again. It was crucial for him to be intubated right away; and because he was struggling, they needed to sedate him. Naty sensed that Ryan wanted to say something, so she asked that Ryan be given a pen and paper. Ryan drew a room. Naty understood that he wanted to be in a private room and not in the ICU. They sedated him after that, never to communicate with any of us ever again.

Pinky, Kaye, and I waited in the hallway of the ER. We noticed a Caucasian couple walking back and forth like they were looking for someone. Finally, they asked us if one of us was Marshi. I nodded my head. The man was a pastor at a church in

Antipolo, Rizal, and they had been asked by Corey, our pastor in Amsterdam, if they could come to Makati Med and pray for us. I was astonished that the pastor and his wife braved the traffic from Antipolo to Makati, a distance of less than 20 km but could take more than two hours, to pray for someone they did not know. It was God's love in action.

Naty texted me to come inside the ER, where the head of the ECMO medical team, Dr. Castro, explained to us what the ECMO machine was and the cost it would entail. An ECMO machine is a life-support machine. It will pump blood from Ryan's body to an artificial lung that will add oxygen to the blood and remove carbon dioxide. The whole process will take place outside the body. It will replace the function of Ryan's own lungs. The ECMO machine will serve as Ryan's lungs because he couldn't and wasn't breathing on his own.

The doctor informed us, "Ryan is qualified for ECMO treatment. He is young; his heart is strong, and he needs help with his lungs. On day 0, the initial cost is one million pesos, and the succeeding days will range between fifty thousand and one hundred thousand pesos daily. If dialysis were needed, it would cost from two hundred fifty thousand to three hundred thousand pesos." (One million pesos was approximately twenty thousand US dollars or seventeen thousand euros.)

I didn't react. I had a blank expression on my face. I had never had a million pesos in my bank account. I knew how much savings we had; and after settling the bill at PDH, the amount was far less than a million pesos.

The doctor inquired, "Are you going for it?"

"Yes, Doc."

He replied, "We had a case in the past where the family, after spending millions of pesos, pulled out on the eighth day because they had no more money. We don't want that to happen. Are you sure?"

I confidently answered, "I don't have the money now, but Ryan is worth so much more than millions. I cannot put a price on his life. Please do everything, Doc, everything. Money should not be a discussion here."

Naty and I rejoined Kaye and Pinky and updated them. I said, "Even if I have to borrow and pay for that debt for the rest of my life, I will do it. God allowed this to happen, so He will provide."

As we waited for the procedure to be completed, Jhaque said, "Ryan will be okay. God could have taken him tonight, but He allowed him to surpass this bump."

I really don't know how I felt at the time. We almost lost Ryan. The kids had no idea that their dad almost died that night. I had no energy to cry. I didn't feel like crying. In fact, I didn't feel anything at all.

PART II

WHILE I WAIT

DAY 8   AUGUST 20, 1ST DAY OF ECMO TREATMENT

I t was 4:00 a.m., and it had been four hours since Ryan was brought to the operating room where the ECMO machine would be connected to Ryan through plastic tubes called cannula. The tubes were to be inserted in large veins and arteries in his legs. We waited... patiently... anxiously...

Help was in short supply. I sent a text blast to family and friends that for the next two weeks (at a minimum, I thought), Ryan would need a companion in the ICU 24/7. The kids also needed to be looked after. I had not been able to spend time with them. There were also administrative tasks I needed to do for Amsterdam and in Manila. I asked for all manpower available and many responded.

The volunteers signed up on their chosen day and shift. They chose either 6:00 a.m. to noon, noon to 6:00 p.m., 6:00 p.m. to midnight, or midnight to 6:00 a.m.

After the ECMO machine was attached to Ryan, I updated my family and friends on Ryan's vital signs and thanked the Lord they were normal and stable. His O2SAT was at 96 percent, and his respiratory rate and blood pressure were normal.

I now turned to the financial aspect. We were told the ECMO treatment was expected to run for ten to fourteen days. The initial cost of the ECMO treatment is one million pesos and the succeeding days will range between fifty thousand and one hundred thousand pesos daily. If dialysis were needed, it would cost between two hundred fifty thousand to three hundred thousand pesos. I estimated our stay at Makati Med would be at least a month, including the period for recovery. The ECMO doctors, Dr. Castro and Dr. Tabora, recommended that if we really wanted to do the ECMO treatment, we should not give up in the middle, because of cost. I confirmed without batting an eyelash. Ryan was worth so much more, and our Heavenly Father, who owns everything, is able and will provide. We told the doctors to do everything they needed to do.

After a long day and evening in PDH and Makati Med, it was time to rest. I sent this short message to family and friends, "Thank you everyone. God has been comforting us through all of you. We feel your prayers, and we return all the love. I will send the hospital visiting policy later. Goodnight at 5:00 a.m."

We peeked through the window of Ryan's ICU room before we left Makati Med. He was fully sedated, so calm, and peaceful. I was happy and relieved to see him finally resting — neither struggling nor having a hard time breathing. Pinky volunteered to stay with Ryan and would stay until she could be relieved by our relatives later in the day. After purchasing the necessary provisions for Pinky, I went home with Naty, Cris, Jhaque, and Kaye. We joked that when Ryan got better, he should wear a mask because his breath would be too expensive to share with others.

When we got home at around 7:00 a.m., I saw Sam's eyes were puffy. I sensed she was sad. She wasn't even smiling. It occurred to me that she must have wondered why all the adults in the house were not at home the previous night. I tried to comfort her and told her about her dad's O2SAT, and that pleased her. I explained to her we might need to stay in the Philippines for another month or so. We talked about temporary schooling and other arrangements.

I felt joy that I could already discuss these things with Sam. I asked her who the giver of life was; she said, "God." I asked her who could take away life; "God," she again said. I told her we could ask God to lend Daddy to us until she got married and had her own kids. That certainly lightened up her mood.

I can't thank God enough for how He had prepared Sam for this. Sam was nine at the time. She understood, and she tried to be strong herself.

Before going to bed that morning, I gave Sam and Shaun a tight hug. In my heart and mind, I had so many things to tell them, but I chose to say nothing. I just hugged them tight and slept.

Later that day, I created an online spreadsheet where everyone could input their available time. Ryan's cousins and nephews made themselves available for the day. Family is truly a blessing!

Since Ryan was fully sedated, I stayed at home during the day to attend to administrative matters. I finally called our Dutch insurance company and informed them of what happened in the Philippines. I called the airlines and informed them of the situation. I was grateful to know they would give a full refund upon submission of the required documents.

What surprised me was a call from a local bank that day. You know those random calls you get from banks and the phone agent would offer a quick cash loan and other promos? They were offering me a one-million-peso cash loan! How did they know? It was only last night when the doctors told me the initial cost of the ECMO treatment was one million pesos; and just a few hours later, here's a bank offering the same amount for a cash loan. I was about to say yes to the offer, but Kaye told me not to avail of it yet. She said God might provide people who could lend money without interest. Kaye had bigger faith than I! Was I rebuked! I told the bank agent to call me after a week.

When we arrived in Manila in mid-July, no one in Ryan's former office knew we were back on holiday. I decided to call Lance, his longtime friend in the office, and tell him about Ryan's situation. He said he would go to Makati Med. When I met Lance at Makati Med, he couldn't believe it was really Ryan in the ICU. When Lance received my call earlier that day, he thought it was a prank call and told his boss about it. They decided that Lance would verify if it were true; and if so, that would be the only time his boss would go to the hospital.

Ryan's former boss and colleagues followed Lance to Makati Med. They were all shocked to see Ryan in that condition. They worked together for nineteen years, and it was only in July 2019 that Ryan moved to a new company in Amsterdam. They said Ryan should join them when the company celebrated its 20th year on September 9. They wanted everyone, including Ryan, to be there.

Meanwhile, Ann arrived from London and went directly to Makati Med with Cris. I was delighted to see Ann, although the circumstances were less than ideal.

Before we left the hospital that day, Ryan's O2SAT was at 100 percent. It was incredible. He was asleep most of the time because he was sedated. We were told that his neurologist would wake him up every day for a certain period to check on his responsiveness, coherence, and alertness.

As of this day, the diagnosis was severe infection. The doctors still didn't know the cause. Dr. Sadili, the pulmonologist and the main attending doctor, repeated that the doctors at PDH did the right things and they did everything they could. Ryan's case was just not giving them enough time, because it was progressing rapidly. With Ryan on the ECMO machine, this gave them time to discover the cause.

We received the first running bill. Aside from the deposit of two hundred thousand pesos we made the night before, we paid at least another half a million pesos. Indeed, God had sent someone who allowed me to use her credit card to pay for that amount.

I was literally taking one day at a time — from Ryan's life, to financial provision, to the availability of people manning the ICU, and to my physical, emotional, psychological, and spiritual strength.

At that point, I had worries at the back of my mind — would Ryan make it? Where would I get the fifteen million pesos to cover the expected hospital costs? How were the kids taking our prolonged absence? I couldn't help but wonder what life would be like at the end of this journey; but I knew many were with us, praying for Ryan's recovery, praying for provision, and praying for the entire family. I chose to believe God was in control of everything.

DAY 9   AUGUST 21, 2ND DAY OF ECMO TREATMENT

A little past 9:00 a.m., my family (Pinky, Naty, Cris, Liezl, Kaye, and Jhaque) and I met with the entire medical team, including the ECMO team, for the first family conference. Each of the specialists discussed the state of the organs affected by Ryan's illness. There were about ten doctors in attendance.

According to the doctors, when Ryan was brought to the Makati Med ER, he was a "dying patient." It was a miracle that he did not die with his oxygen saturation level at 40, his BP at 60/40, and his respiratory rate at 40 (the normal range is between 14 and 18).

Ryan had a severe case of pneumonia, but they didn't know yet what caused it. They ran all the tests, and all yielded negative results. While they were able to isolate only Adenovirus (the virus that causes common cold and cough), they didn't think it was the cause of Ryan's sickness. The doctors said they would continue to investigate.

One of the doctors asked me if I was Ryan's first girlfriend. "No, but I'm the first wife," was my answer. I knew why they asked that question. That's why I answered it that way. If they knew Ryan, they would know that he believed in sex only in the context of marriage. It didn't matter if he had girlfriends before he married me, what mattered was that I was his only wife.

They directed the next question to Pinky, being the sister. They asked her if Ryan was "promiscuous" when he was single. Pinky readily answered no. More than her reply, I was relieved they didn't ask me that question. If they did, I wouldn't have been able to answer it because I didn't know what the word "promiscuous" meant. I thought it would have been embarrassing and funny.

The doctors continued to say they considered the fact that we lived in Amsterdam. Of course, we all know what the "red light" district in Amsterdam is known for. They, however, reported that Ryan tested negative for HIV. That was his second negative result; the first was at PDH. When I heard that, I asked myself, if he tested negative, why then did they have to ask all those questions? Ryan was a faithful husband and a faithful follower of Christ.

Before the family conference came to an end, Pinky asked if she could close the conference in prayer. She thanked God for the team of doctors attending to Ryan. She prayed for wisdom, knowledge, and good health for them so they could best know how to help Ryan.

After we prayed, I approached Dr. Sadili and thanked her. She embraced me and asked if I wanted to see Ryan. We walked to the next room where Ryan was. I stood beside his bed, touched his arm, and gently said, "Dad, I am here." I told him his former boss and colleagues came to visit the day before, that we missed him already, the kids missed him so much, and that we would always be there for him. Before leaving, I reminded him of what we had agreed on — for him to pray and fight. I told him I loved him.

It was the second day on the ECMO machine, and we had to pay the hospital another half a million pesos. In his faithfulness, God provided through a friend who allowed me to use her credit card.

Since Ryan would be sedated for the rest of the day, we went home after lunch to be with the kids. Friends and family came to visit Ryan; many volunteered to be with him. The doctor told

Pinky that Ryan shed a tear when they told him I had come to see him.

Ryan underwent hemodialysis to support the kidneys while he was on intravenous medication. He was also given a transfusion of one unit of blood for anemia.

Papa, on the other hand, had already been discharged from PDH. Now we could all focus on taking care of Ryan.

Late that afternoon, I asked Kaye to take me to a nearby Starbucks. There I paused for a moment to reflect on what was happening. I had a much-needed cry; I just had to release the heaviness in my heart. When I felt better, I called Sam's school in Amsterdam, her after-school care, Shaun's daycare, and our Dutch insurance company. Each phone call was difficult as I needed to stay composed so I could explain to the person on the other line why I called and the current state of Ryan's health. The conversation with our Dutch insurance company was not encouraging. I was told that we had a basic plan only, and if ever we would receive something, it wouldn't be a substantial amount.

During dinner, I went to the bedroom ahead of Naty, Kaye, Jhaque, Ann, and Cris. Unknown to me, they talked about helping me raise funds to cover Ryan's estimated hospital costs. Kaye asked if it was possible for the ladies to raise one million pesos each. With the daily hospital bill, one million pesos was the new one hundred thousand pesos. Kaye also suggested doing a crowdfunding and asked Ann to check with me if I was fine with the idea. Ann relayed it to me, and I agreed. That was when The Incredible Ryan Facebook page was conceived. First, we needed to inform friends and loved ones of the situation.

Indeed, at the time, I felt the value of money diminished. In just two days, our running bill was almost two million pesos. Since when has one million pesos been mentioned so casually in the family? We witnessed God's miracle in Ryan's life each day. He had been sending people whom we hadn't met before to bless and pray for us. I continued to hang on, to hold on to His promises, and to ask everyone to storm the heavens with our cries for God to heal Ryan and make him healthy once more.

"For nothing will be impossible with God." (Luke 1:37 English Standard Version)

In the morning, Pinky and I went to see Ryan during the thirty-minute sedation holiday. To check Ryan's neurologic status, they did a daily sedation holiday (his neurologist would stop the sedation for about twenty to thirty minutes a day to allow Ryan to become alert). She read Psalm 23, and we sang "Lover of My Soul" to him. He raised his eyebrows, opened his eyes, and moved his feet! Those were very encouraging signs to us! We told Ryan what day it was and the time of the day. We also told him not to be afraid if he couldn't move his whole body because the doctors had temporarily paralyzed him to protect all the tubes connected to him. In between tears, Pinky tried to encourage him.

When it was my turn to talk to him, I said hi. And fighting back tears, I held his arm tightly and told him I missed him. How was I to express everything I wanted to say in so short a time? It was one of those moments when I had so many things in my heart and on my mind, but not many words came out. If Ryan were awake, he would have understood the tears in my eyes.

Ryan was sedated again until the next morning.

I stayed in the ICU with friends who visited that day. Corey had asked another pastor who was doing his ministry in the Philippines, to come to Makati Med to pray for us. It was such a blessing to have brothers and sisters in the Lord as a source of comfort, love, and encouragement. A family friend sent siopao (steamed pork bun) and nacho chips to Makati Med for the volunteers. God had been sending people to bless those who were blessing us.

Pinky went to their house in Taytay for the first time since she arrived in Manila, to tell Mama Nila of Ryan's situation. Pinky gently broke the news to Mama Nila that Ryan was at the ICU of Makati Med with pneumonia, and that he had a low oxygen supply. She mentioned that Ryan was connected to an apparatus to keep him relaxed and rested. She wanted to save the news about the ECMO treatment and dialysis for her next update. When Mama Nila cried, Pinky encouraged Mama Nila to continue praying for the doctors that they would discover the cause of Ryan's illness.

That night I found myself alone in the dining area. The running bill was on the dining table. I was silently thinking how we could possibly cover the costs, as every day hundreds of thousands were being added to the bill. My mind must have wandered so far that I didn't notice Sam approaching; and before I knew it, she was already reading the hospital bill.

Sam asked, "What?! They did all of these tests to Dad?"

I just nodded my head.

Sam replied, "Two million two hundred thousand pesos?! Do we have this money, Mommy?"

"No," I replied with a half-smile.

"How about your euro money?"

"No, we don't have that much, Sam."

"So, how do we intend to pay for this?"

"I don't know. I'm still asking God."

Then she left.

As I sat for a little while, I received a WhatsApp message from a brother in faith in Amsterdam. His text was such a rebuke to my doubting heart. His message read, "Marshi, please, you have to believe completely and flush out and don't entertain any doubt . . .

Receive the healing with grace regardless of the doctors. As He alone gives them wisdom."

I believe that was the defining moment. I sincerely asked God for forgiveness for praying yet doubting. It was between me and God. While people thought I was so strong and my faith was unwavering, God saw the doubts and worries in my heart and mind. I was ashamed of myself. From that time on, I asked, and I believed. Little did I know He was preparing me for even greater challenges in the days to come.

DAY 11   AUGUST 23, 4TH DAY OF ECMO TREATMENT

On this day, Ryan didn't have a sedation holiday, so I stayed at home while family and friends stayed with him at the ICU. Pinky remained in Taytay with Mama. Pastors and churchmates went to their house and prayed for and with them.

Our household members, including the kids, were starting to get sick. Some had fevers; others had coughs. Shaun had a fever and pneumonia; therefore, we decided to have everyone x-rayed.

Late in the afternoon, Naty and I took Shaun to PDH for admission. We initially stayed at the ER for a few hours and Shaun behaved the entire time. He just sat on my lap while the doctors were taking his vital signs and asking questions. Kaye and Charo later joined us at PDH.

I now had two patients. I had only one thing to say to the Lord, "Lord, you said you will not give us anything beyond what we can bear. You know my limits."

We breathed a sigh of relief when we saw that all x-ray results were normal. Although Sam's x-ray was also normal, the doctors acted on the side of caution and started her on antibiotics.

I fully dedicated myself to Shaun since he needed me more. I was confident that the rest of the family and my friends would be with Ryan. It was one of the biggest blessings we enjoyed at the time. God just touched the hearts of many to volunteer to be with Ryan.

There was indeed no scarcity of acts of love and kindness — many friends and family took turns staying overnight at the ICU. Even those who worked night shifts volunteered to man the

ICU after their work. A friend, her husband, and their two kids spent their Sunday morning at the ICU. A stranger who learned of The Incredible Ryan story from a friend signed up on the Google sheet many times to stay at the ICU.

This had become our journey together, not only mine, not only of the family.

And God, in His infinite wisdom, had allowed all things to happen; and by His amazing grace, we held on and continued to hope for the best.

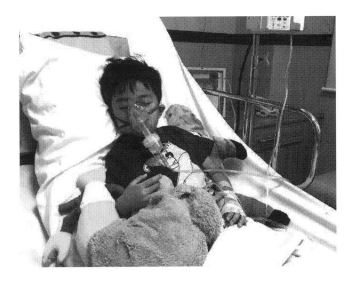

After a long wait at the ER of PDH, Shaun was finally able to rest with Diglet and Sharklet, his beloved toys. He has accumulated seven Diglets.

I t was the second family conference. Kaye, Naty, Pinky, Paolo, and I went to Makati Med to attend, while Jhaque and Ann went to PDH to take care of Shaun.

The medical team updated us on Ryan's overall condition and on each affected organ. Ryan had severe pneumonia, which led to sepsis and acute respiratory distress syndrome. The microorganism causing it remained unknown despite extensive laboratory tests.

Ryan had an acute kidney injury and was on continuous renal replacement therapy, a dialysis that ran for 24 hours a day, to allow his kidneys to rest and hopefully recover within a few months. He was on the third day of his dialysis to detoxify the blood and release excess fluids. He had also developed an acute liver injury due to the infection and all the medication that was being given to him. A new doctor had been added to the team to address this problem.

As of this day, he responded, obeyed simple commands, and opened his eyes. He also shed a tear. Since the parameters would go down during the sedation holiday (for example his O2SAT would go down to 80s), they scheduled the sedation holiday every three days instead of every day.

Ryan's heart was functioning well. They did a 2D echocardiogram the day before and would do it every five days. His x-ray result showed a very slight improvement, which, at this stage, was already great news for us. He had no problem with his gastrointestinal tract.

It was a good conference. I had never appreciated our body organs as much as I did that day. Understanding how one organ affects the other organs and the rest of the body reminded me of how great God is, how much He loves mankind, and that He created us in His image.

After lunch, I went back to PDH to take care of Shaun. Sam was left at home with her cousins. I wondered what she must have felt at that time — her dad and brother were both sick in the hospital, and her mom juggled her time to be with all of them. I missed her so much, and I longed for the time when all this would come to an end and we could go on with our normal lives.

I continued to update our family and friends through The Incredible Ryan Facebook page. Below is what I wrote in my update.

a. *Watchers*
   Please bring a jacket to keep yourselves warm. Refer to the Google sheet to sign up. Again, we thank you with all our love.

b. *Blood Donors*
   Blood type needed is O+. For now, we only need you to sign up on the Google sheet until further notice. Thank you.

c. *Financial Support*
   To those who have helped financially, I pray that God will be the one to bless you abundantly in return. Thank you.

Our Dutch insurance company has already reached out to Makati Med. They will let us know how much of the cost they will cover after evaluating the medical abstract.

We will create a crowdfunding account only after the Dutch insurance company's evaluation. We do not want to raise more than what we need. The doctors gave us a ballpark figure of fifteen million pesos. By faith we will endure until the end, whatever it takes.

d. Prayer Items

1. Doctors and all medical staff
    For wisdom to know who the enemy in this battle is. For strength to fight until the very end.

2. Family
    For faith to endure and to never waver in trusting God who holds all things in His hands.

3. Friends all over the world
    To pray without ceasing until we see the completion of God's plan in Ryan's life.

4. Insurance
    For the Dutch insurance company to cover part, if not all the costs. For sustained provision until Ryan's full recovery.

5. *Marshi*

    Wisdom for me on how to deal with our life in Amsterdam that is now temporarily put on hold, e.g., house rent, Sam's school, Shaun's day care, our responsibilities at work, etc. Wisdom on how to move on as we go through this experience. Wisdom on how to meet the needs of the kids as I support Ryan. We've been taking it one day at a time. Praise God that his mercies are new every morning.

"We are hard pressed on every side but not crushed; ..." (2 Corinthians 4:8 NIV)

"...For the battle is not yours, but God's." (2 Chronicles 20:15b NIV)

*****

I cried every now and then. I was emotionally and physically tired and so was the rest of the family.

The God we believed in yesterday, when things were going fine, is the same God who loves us now in these trying times; and He is the same God tomorrow when everything will be all right.

Hebrews 13:8 (NIV) says, "Jesus Christ is the same yesterday and today and forever."

Sam kept herself entertained at home while
the rest of her family was at the hospital.

DAY 13 AUGUST 25, 6TH DAY OF ECMO TREATMENT

The whole family attended the 35th anniversary celebration of Christ's Commission Fellowship (our church in Manila) and planned to visit Ryan after the service. Ryan was not alone as many family and friends spent their entire Sunday at the ICU.

Pinky attended the worship service with Mama Nila at Emmanuel Baptist Church in Taytay. She gave a testimony at the service and updated everyone about Ryan. She also sang and dedicated to Ryan a song she composed when she had a miscarriage a few months earlier. One of the lines in the song says, "If in this trial you feel I seem distant and silent… It's because I'm holding you." This truth comforted me.

Shaun's high fever had not gone down since the night before. The doctors were already discussing whether we should transfer Shaun to Makati Med because it was possible that his case might be like that of Ryan's. Although Shaun tested negative for dengue and typhoid fever, the doctors continued to monitor him because of his high-grade fever.

I was so blessed to see my friends Chiqui, Dr. Galvez, and his wife Belinda at PDH for the first time since we arrived in Manila. They were truly a source of comfort after all the family had been through the past weeks. Liezl and Charo also came to visit the little boy.

At around 11:00 p.m., I received a text message from Maricel and Chilet, who were the volunteers at the ICU. They said Mickey, a former ECMO patient at Makati Med, would be visiting Ryan tomorrow. Mickey was sort of a "celebrity" in the ECMO world of Makati Med. He was the first patient in Makati Med to undergo the ECMO treatment and recover from his illness. His story was truly inspiring. Meeting him would give us an opportunity to ask so many questions we had about his experience while on the ECMO machine, his recovery period, and the current state of his health. Meeting him was something we had hoped for, and I was grateful that he would visit.

Kaye and I stayed with Shaun that Sunday evening. It was a long night for us — Shaun's fever still had not gone down.

DAY 14   AUGUST 26, 7TH DAY OF ECMO TREATMENT

Kaye flew back to Hong Kong after extending her stay in Manila for a week. My brother Paul also returned to Cebu after flying in last Saturday. He spent the weekend with us, which I really appreciated as he rarely visited Manila. I wished I could keep them both in Manila, but they had work responsibilities.

I sent a message to the family to encourage them to hold on and keep on. They had been a tremendous blessing to me and the kids. In my text, I said:

Good morning, family. We are now on day seven of ECMO treatment. It dawned on me that day fourteen is next Monday. This is the week we expect great things from God. I am both excited and afraid, but I am at peace. Let's hang on. God is good.

This also means that by Monday, we should have raised eight to ten million pesos. I will call the Dutch insurance company today and we will create the crowdfunding account as needed. The Lord has already touched the hearts of many; I know He will provide. I want you to know that I am very, very thankful to all of you, and we love you so dearly.

Jhaque and Ann relieved me at PDH as I had to be home by 10:00 a.m. to meet the buyer of our car. I was able to sell our Toyota Innova at a good price. The proceeds would help defray the hospital expenses. The Lord sent the right people to connect me to the buyer at the right time.

Pinky went to Makati Med after spending the weekend in Taytay and had a chance to talk to Dr. Sadili. Dr. Sadili continued to study and research Ryan's case, and had a teleconference call with a colleague in New Zealand. Dr. Sadili and the team were adopting a new strategy — they started to give Ryan vitamins and corticosteroids. She was very hopeful that this treatment would be helpful.

I had intended to meet Pinky at Makati Med so we could both meet Mickey in the afternoon; however, around lunch time, the doctors at PDH advised us to transfer Shaun to Makati Med.

Ann took Sam and her cousins skating in the afternoon. It meant a lot to me whenever a family member or friend spent time with Sam. At least I knew one Brozo family member was somewhere enjoying herself.

After their skating, a cousin picked up Sam at the mall. Sam would spend a few nights at their place. I greatly appreciated my cousin's gesture and was so happy that Sam would be preoccupied in the coming days.

Just before we transferred Shaun to Makati Med, my friends Jen and Vera arrived at PDH. They originally volunteered to take care of Shaun that afternoon since it was a public holiday. Jen and Vera joined me and Naty, as we took Shaun to Makati Med.

As we waited for our turn, I sat in the ER with Shaun on my lap. At the time, I was devoid of emotions. I was not feeling anything. Silently, I told God, "Lord, there is only one ECMO machine in this hospital. There is no room for Shaun," as if God needed to be told. "Lord, you know that one family member on the ECMO machine is already too much. Two would be impossible to bear," as if God didn't know.

We waited in the ER for more than six hours before we were transferred to a private room. I was grateful to God because Shaun didn't give us any difficulty. A family friend brought balloons to cheer Shaun up, while Jhaque and Vera made sure we had burgers and fries for our dinner; not the healthiest of food, but something that cheered us up. Shaun was on the 5th floor, while Ryan was on the 4th floor. If there was anything good about that, I was just one floor away from Ryan the whole time.

Lord...

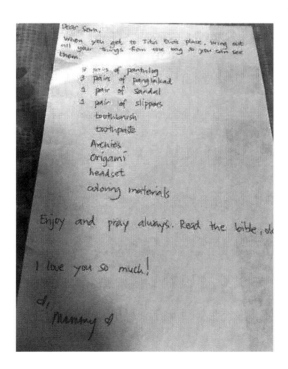

My love note to Sam with my instructions
for her stay at her aunt's place.

Ryan remained stable on life support. The family conference originally scheduled on this day was moved to the morning of the following day. They would do a brain scan (EEG) and 2D echocardiogram.

His liver was getting better with medication, although he was still on dialysis. When Ryan went on a sedation holiday the day before, his O2SAT went down to 80s after ten minutes, which indicated that his lungs were still far from functioning on their own. I asked family and friends to continue storming the heavens for Ryan's healing. Though it seemed that time was not on our side, I knew God's time is always perfect, not too early, never late.

Shaun, on the other hand, improved. In the past twelve hours he hadn't had a fever. I thanked and praised God for the improvement in Shaun's health. I continued to pray that Shaun's case was different from Ryan's and that he would be discharged as soon as possible.

Sam was still at our cousin's house, where she could have some normalcy in her life for a few days.

I was blessed by the outpouring of support and help from family and friends. Many asked for my bank account details and the crowdfunding account, which we had not yet set up. I still needed to check with the Dutch insurance company as to how much (if any) they would cover. There were a lot of administrative things I neglected to do in the past days, especially after Shaun got sick. And with two patients, we needed more manpower and volunteer watchers for Ryan. It was amazing that God kept all of us healthy while taking care of Ryan and Shaun.

The doctors said they were doing everything medically possible to treat Ryan, but Ryan was not showing any significant improvement. In fact, they almost lost Ryan yesterday. I realized each day we had Ryan was already a blessing. The doctors recognized Ryan's case required a "higher intervention." Dr. Sadili called for my sister Naty to come to her clinic and said Ryan needed divine intervention. The doctors requested that pastors see Ryan that day and pray over him. Many pastors heeded our request and came to pray for Ryan.

*****

Early in Ryan's career, he expressed his desire to become a pastor; but since Pinky was already a full-time church worker and married to a pastor, the thought of having Pinky and Ryan spend their lives in ministry did not seem like a good idea. At that time, Ryan's parents were still paying the mortgage on their house and were relying on Ryan to pay off the loan and support the family. Ryan needed a well-paying job.

Ryan accepted Mama's advice and said that he would work in the corporate world so he could financially provide for the family. Ryan worked in a start-up company where he spent the next 19 years of his career as a software architect.

Fast forward to 2018. The family moved to Amsterdam; we found a small but growing Bible-believing church. Our family was part of the missional community serving in the city center of Amsterdam. Our Senior Pastor, Corey, talked to Ryan and asked if

Ryan were willing to lead a missional community that the church would create for Amstelveen, where we were living. Ryan said he would pray about it.

Sam is an intelligent and mature child. We talked to her about serious issues affecting our family and always included her in decisions that might have an impact on her. One day, Ryan asked Sam how she would feel if he decided to become a pastor. Sam was excited about it. "Then you'll be just like Tito Corey; Mom would be like Tita Kaylee; and I would be like Lyla." She compared our would-be family life to that of Corey's family. I just listened to the two as they talked. In my mind, I wasn't ready for Ryan to become a full-time church worker. That possibility scared me because I wouldn't want to be placed in a position where all eyes were on us. I knew we are called to be holy as God is Holy, but I also knew I would fail time and again. I was not ready to say, "Yes, Lord, here I am, use me in any way You please." But I kept it to myself.

Fast forward again . . . I was sitting in Makati Med. My mind wandered back to that part of Ryan's life when he wanted to become a pastor, to that conversation between Ryan and Sam. I felt guilty. If it were God's plan for Ryan to serve in the ministry, how could I desire otherwise? In my conversations with Pinky and their cousins, I realized I may have unintentionally hindered God's plan in Ryan's life. According to Pinky, Mama also felt she had prevented Ryan from fulfilling God's plan in his life.

At that moment, I became hopeful. I thought all this was happening as part of God's plan for Ryan to do what God had called him to do — to work in the ministry. Pinky and I honestly believed in our hearts that when Ryan recovered, God would accomplish His purpose in Ryan's life.

"but they who wait for the LORD shall renew their strength; they shall mount up with wings like eagles; they shall run and not be weary; they shall walk and not faint." (Isaiah 40:31 ESV)

DAY 16   AUGUST 28, 9TH DAY OF ECMO TREATMENT

We had the third family conference; and the medical team reported that Ryan's heart and brain remained in normal condition, while his liver was being managed. His lungs continued to receive support from the ECMO machine, and his kidneys were on continuous renal replacement therapy.

Of all the tests that had been done, which included blood and sputum culture, oral swab, and bronchial lavage, they isolated only adenovirus, a kind of virus that causes pneumonia, and Acinetobacter, a kind of bacteria that Ryan acquired in Makati Med.

The doctors continued to address the health issues and waited for Ryan's body to respond. The latest chest x-ray showed a slight clearing, but this had not been translated physiologically since his oxygen requirement was still high. This meant the primary function of the lungs was still compromised; and the provision of oxygen to reach at least the 95th percentile requirement was still dependent on the machine.

Meanwhile, Shaun had been without fever for thirty-six hours. I was happy, praying, and hopeful Shaun would be discharged the next day.

I updated my family and friends about the blood type that Ryan needed; and asked those who were able and willing to donate, to sign up on our Google sheet or go straight to the blood donation center of Makati Med. It was amazing how God touched other people to help through their blood donation. There were those who we did not know, but were friends of friends, who went to Makati Med to donate their blood. There were those who tried but were not able to donate because they did not meet the qualifications. Some didn't even text or call us, but just went there. It was God moving in our midst.

I finally heard from our Dutch insurance company. They would only cover up to a maximum of eight thousand euros, approximately less than half a million pesos. While the amount was nothing compared to the need, I was still grateful no matter how little it was. The family did not have fifteen million pesos, but God owns everything. I knew He would provide. We decided to go ahead and create a crowdfunding account. God might provide through others whose hearts He would touch and move to help.

Ann and Kaye created the GoGetFunding account, with Ann as campaign owner and Kaye as funds captain. We provided GBP, Euro, HKD, AUD, and PHP bank accounts so family and friends could donate through their local currency. We also asked them to deposit directly to the bank accounts to avoid the stiff administrative fee. Indeed, God blessed us through family and friends.

*****

Sam had not yet visited Ryan; she said she would only visit once her dad was awake. On this day, she asked if Ryan was awake and if she could go and see him because she wanted to show her dad a YouTube video about how the movie *Spider-Man: Far From Home* should have ended. Ryan and Sam loved Marvel movies. Oftentimes, Ryan would show Sam YouTube videos of how certain Marvel movies should have ended. They shared similar interests — movies, coding, drawing, games — they had their own world. Sam's innocence to everything that was happening to her dad broke my heart. How I hoped this would soon be over.

I had not given up on Ryan. Up to that very moment, I continued to plead to God to lend Ryan to me, Sam, and Shaun for many more quality years. I cried out to Him to grant the desires of my heart. I was at peace holding on.

I asked for prayers — for life and healing. I asked that when we pray, we should expect great things from God, never doubting.

In His time, He will work on each of our hearts and prepare us. God never sleeps. He hears us.

DAY 17 AUGUST 29, 10TH DAY OF ECMO TREATMENT

There was no sedation holiday scheduled on this day; nonetheless, Pinky and I separately spent a few minutes with Ryan.

When it was my turn, I told him I had not yet surrendered, and that we, together with Sam and Shaun, were waiting for him to come back to us. I tried to humor him that he had been lying down there for a long time now; it was already unfair. I told him he needed to shave. I told him so many casual things. Most importantly, I told him I hoped he had already spent time talking to God.

I knew Ryan could hear me because he tried to move his lips and tongue as if he wanted to say something. He moved his fingers on his right hand, and he kept moving his foot, too! I was wondering, though, how he was doing it when he was fully sedated. I was very sure those were not involuntary movements. That gave me so much hope. He was alive. He was awake. He was with me. He heard me and he tried to respond. God knew I needed some encouragement that day.

God sent more good news! Later that day I got an email from our Dutch insurance company, which I wasn't expecting to receive. The email read:

Dear Mrs. Brozo,

Thank you for your reply.

We have been informed that at this moment we can inform you, we will issue a guarantee with a maximum coverage of € 35.526,13 (thirty-five thousand five hundred twenty-six Euro and thirteen cent) à via OAND currency converter PHP 2,059,280.

The final maximum coverage can be calculated after discharge and receival of the medical notes.

ONVZ covers the Dutch price, based on diagnosis, specific examinations etc. See attachment for explanation.

We remain in contact with you.

We wish your husband a good recovery.

*****

From five hundred thousand pesos, they were now covering up to two million pesos! I didn't even ask for it. God must have touched their hearts and used them to meet our financial needs. Because of this amazing development, we lowered our target amount in GoGetFunding from fifteen million to thirteen million pesos. Everything that was happening was beyond me. I could only rely on God in complete surrender.

Sam visited Shaun in Makati Med, but she didn't see her dad. It was not time yet.

Ryan's x-ray result on this day showed some improvement compared to the previous day. The x-ray result showed more dark regions. Air on an x-ray looks dark; so, when the lungs are clear and healthy, they should look quite dark.

God continued to show His love for us, despite everything. There was never a moment when I questioned the goodness of God. His grace really helped me to keep on and continue entrusting the unknown future to the One who sees it.

On this day, Kaye flew back to Manila while Jhaque went back to Leyte after extending her stay for almost two weeks. Kaye had planned to indefinitely stay in and work remotely from Manila to be with my family and me.

It was Kaye's turn to take Sam out. They went to Sip & Gogh to paint, one of Sam's favorite things to do. After their date, they proceeded to Makati Med, not to see Ryan, but to take Shaun home.

Shaun's x-ray result was clear, and he could go home later in the afternoon. Praise God! It was such a relief to know that his case was not the same as Ryan's. I really thanked God for healing Shaun. Now we could just focus on Ryan again. Ryan was no longer on sedation, but he was still in a deep sleep. The doctors said this was unusual, but they were giving it more time.

We started praying and asked everyone to pray with us for Ryan to wake up soon. As it turned out, my "talk" with Ryan when he responded to me by moving his foot, fingers, tongue, and lips, was my last "interaction" with him...

DAY 19 AUGUST 31, 12TH DAY OF ECMO TREATMENT

We were now on day 12 of ECMO treatment. We needed a ray of hope at that point and we were greatly encouraged that day.

Below is the good news I posted on the Incredible Ryan Facebook page after the family conference:

1. *Heart medicines are off. His heart is functioning well.*
2. *Kidneys remain the same, with no further deterioration. They are still on continuous renal replacement therapy.*
3. *Liver enzymes are going down, which is good. Sedation and paralysis medicines are off. This should help the liver to recover.*
4. *Lungs are clearing up, praise God! If you look at the photo below, the left x-ray was taken on August 27, while the right x-ray was taken on August 30. The darker the image, the more air there is. Let us pray that the improvement continues and that the lungs will not regress.*
5. *Insulin at minimum level, which is also a good sign.*

Urgent prayer items:

1. *Brain*
   Ryan has been off sedation for more than twenty-four hours already, but he has not yet woken up. The doctors need to know whether there is bleeding in his brain. An EEG will be done today. A CT scan is not feasible as there

are many machines and tubes attached to him. If they have a portable ultrasound machine at Makati Med, they plan to do an ultrasound bedside. Please pray that there is no bleeding.

2. *Tracheostomy*

    Since he has been intubated for two weeks now, they will do a tracheostomy on Monday at 8:00 a.m. Please pray for a successful procedure as this will be done bedside. Pray also that not much blood will be lost. Thank you to all those who have donated blood today. We received the information that we have already enough for Monday. Praise God!

*****

Our faith was tested each day. There came a point when I wanted to ask, "Why Lord?" and "Until when Lord?" But God is good all the time. I chose to trust in His sovereignty. That was the only way to endure this journey up to the very end. I prayed that all those praying would not get tired of praying, hoping, and supporting. The Lord gave me and my family strength and comfort knowing that we were not alone in this battle.

The next family conference was on September 3.

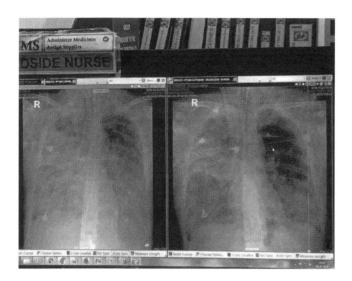

Photo of Ryan's x-ray results. The x-rays
were done three days apart.

Early that morning, I received a request from the doctors to see them ASAP because they needed to talk to me. I, along with Naty and Pinky, arrived at Makati Med after 7:00 a.m. We met Dr. Sadili and the ECMO team, Dr. Castro and Dr. Tabora, at the Makati Med cafeteria. Ryan had been bleeding since 3:00 a.m. in his lower gastrointestinal tract (300cc), which continued until 7:00 a.m., at which time the doctors were able to contain it at 40cc.

I haven't mentioned yet, Dr. Castro is also a follower of Christ. It gave me additional comfort that we were connected by our faith in God, who was and continued to be in control of everything that was happening. I would like to believe that our testimonies touched the hearts of the entire team of doctors and nurses.

Praise God because Ryan's bleeding was brought under control; and it was localized and not general, which could have been fatal. Ryan also started to spontaneously breathe on his own! The doctors would wean him off the ECMO life support on this day. His bleeding needed to stop so the doctors could wean him at a normal pace.

The doctors planned the following: if Ryan would wake up, they would do a tracheostomy at his bedside the next morning. If he woke up responsive, that would mean there was no damage in his brain. If not, he, with all the many machines and monitors attached to him, would be moved to the CT scan room on the ground floor to check for a brain hemorrhage. The planned move would not be an easy task, and our prayer was for Ryan to wake up. With Ryan awake, the tracheostomy would be much easier to execute.

Many blood donors came to the hospital. To say I was overwhelmed was an understatement. Some weren't allowed to donate because they failed to meet the qualifications (e.g., the donor consumed alcohol the night before or was underweight). Just the same, we were grateful for their willingness to help the family. We informed everyone through the Facebook page that we had already more than enough blood supply for the day.

God provided for us in so many ways. Someone who owns a laundry shop washed our weeks' worth of laundry for free! I had no time to take care of these things, and God sent people to take care of even the smallest things.

Many people came and prayed. The hallway outside of Ryan's room was sometimes filled with friends and visitors. At times, we literally knelt in the ICU hallways and pleaded to God to wake Ryan up. Of all the rooms in the ICU section, Ryan's was the busy one. We were grateful the hospital never asked us to limit the number of visitors at a given time.

We had planned for a discreet vacation in Manila — no social media posts while we were in Asia for six weeks. But God had another plan. He caused schoolmates in elementary, high school, and college to come to Makati Med. Former co-workers, churchmates, and relatives visited. God sent all of them to help us man the ICU, donate blood, pray for Ryan, comfort the family, and bless us financially. He never left us alone.

After dinner, I asked Naty what she thought of Ryan's case. Her feeling was Ryan would survive but might be in a coma for some time. If that happened, she said she would be willing to take care of Ryan while we returned to Amsterdam. She would dedicate a room in their house for Ryan and have a private nurse attend to him; and we could just come back to Manila when Ryan woke up. I was so moved by her selflessness. I told her God knows my limits. I prayed and was praying for Ryan to be alive and be healthy. If I was going to ask God for something, I was going to ask for the best.

"For from him and through him and to him are all things...." (Romans 11:36 ESV)

Blessed be the name of the Lord!

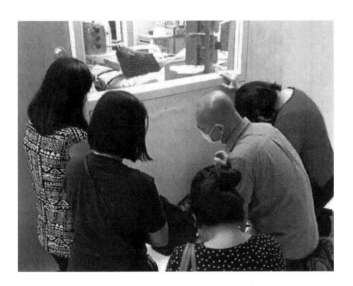

One of those days when friends prayed in
the ICU hallway of Makati Med.

Day 14/14.

I had been praying for the right moment to bring Sam to the ICU to visit her dad. I knew I wouldn't be able to spend much time with the children while Ryan was in the hospital. I feared those moments when Sam was left alone and would worry about her dad, and that I wouldn't be there for her.

But this day was special. It was time to see her dad. She finally had the courage to see Ryan. I brought Sam to Makati Med.

Initially, we just stayed outside the ICU and peeked through the glass window to Ryan's room. She saw her dad, with many tubes attached to him. She saw all the machines and monitors surrounding her dad.

She quietly asked what each machine was for. I tried to explain how the ECMO machine worked. I knew this was hard for her to understand. She just nodded her head. I wasn't sure if Sam realized how sick her dad was.

After much convincing, we went inside the ICU but just stood outside Ryan's room. Sam didn't want to go near Ryan because she wasn't comfortable around all the tubes attached to her dad.

I felt relief that Sam had finally seen her dad and the seriousness of his condition. I wasn't sure what was running through Sam's mind. She didn't want to talk about her feelings at the time. It took Sam three months before she opened her heart about her dad's death.

At nine, Sam was a picture of calmness. Undoubtedly, she loved and adored her dad, but she kept her emotions to herself.

Perhaps, Sam was just as innocent as she appears. Perhaps, her child-like faith kept her going. How I wished we could cry out together, hug each other and comfort one another. It would have been easier if we both had the same emotional response to what was happening. It would have made my role as a mom a bit easier to know exactly how to comfort her. Perhaps, it was one way of God telling me not to worry about her, because she would be fine. I hope so. Later, Sam said that if the time came that she didn't know what to specifically pray for anymore, she would just ask God to heal her dad.

The Bible comforted me with the truth that God would never allow something beyond what I could bear. That day, I was reminded that this truth also applied to Sam. God would not give her anything beyond what she, a nine-year old, could bear.

*****

The tracheostomy was deferred due to the bleeding in Ryan's GI tract. Ryan had to wake up! We prayed so hard for God to preserve Ryan's brain, for God to wake him up that day as he had been sleeping for almost three days now.

Late in the afternoon, the doctors decided to do a CT scan, even if it meant bringing Ryan and all the machines to the ground floor. They studied how they could bring Ryan's bed, with all the machines hanging on the sides of the bed, to the CT scan room. They measured the length and width of the bed with everything attached to it and made sure that everything would fit in the elevator. It was going to be an especially important procedure, and they planned every detail of it. I was incredibly grateful to the

"Incredible Ryan" team of doctors and all the medical staff. They were amazing!

We waited while they prepared to move Ryan. When they were about to pass the ICU hallway, we were all lined up. It was quite a sight. The team walked briskly past us while pushing Ryan's bed. The elevator, which had been on standby for almost an hour, took them to the ground floor. We all followed and stayed outside the CT scan room.

We thought it would take a long time, so Kaye and Bambi went out to buy hot drinks for everyone. Just as they came back, the medical team came out of the CT scan room. As they walked past us, Dr. Castro looked back and told Naty that there was bleeding in Ryan's brain. They walked so quickly that we didn't have the chance to ask anything. They took Ryan back to the ICU, while we all followed behind.

After 10:00 pm., Dr. Castro and Dr. Tabora joined us at the waiting area outside Ryan's room, which had become my home for the past three weeks. The CT scan result showed 21 ml of blood in the brain stem of Ryan. The next family conference was scheduled the following day to discuss the succeeding steps.

We ended the extremely long day by blessing the Lord's name and still declaring His goodness and faithfulness.

At that moment, I was in complete surrender to God and God alone. I did not feel defeated. Some cried when we regrouped after having been told by Dr. Castro of the result. I couldn't bring myself to cry. For some reason, I wanted to continue believing that God would answer our prayers as we wanted Him to — to bring Ryan back to us. If it is His will, the time to cry will come. But this wasn't the time yet for me. For Sam and Shaun, I continued to hope that their dad would live and be well.

Sam's first visit to her dad at the ICU of Makati Med.

Family and friends regrouped and prayed with
the ECMO doctors after a CT scan on Ryan
showed a bleeding in his brain stem.

PART III

AND I COMPLETELY SURRENDER

That early morning, my dear sister Ann flew back to London after being with us in Manila for the last two weeks. She said she would come back when Ryan was awake again…

We braced ourselves for the fifth family conference. Pinky, Naty, Kaye, Cris, and Liezl joined me.

When we entered the room, everyone was silent. It was quite different from the previous family conferences. The mood was somber, to say the least. We took our seats without saying much. In the past conferences, the doctors carried on with the conversations they were having before we arrived; or Naty and Liezl, being doctors also, would chat with some of the members of the medical team.

In all the family conferences, the pulmonologist, Dr. Sadili always led the discussion — she would open and close it. She was the main attending physician, after all. But certain specialists would dominate the discussion depending on the organ or organs that had problems at the time. There was the cardiologist, the infectious disease specialist, and the nephrologist. In this conference, it was the turn of the neurologist.

We were told that, based on the CT scan, Ryan was clinically brain dead. I asked the neurologist, "Doc, was there ever a case when a clinically brain dead person woke up?" She shook her head. There wasn't much to say. This wasn't where we wanted to be on day 15. By this time, we hoped to have been moved to a private room.

I was asked if they should resuscitate should Ryan arrest. Without a blink I said yes. Then there was silence. It was a long silence. And during that time the prompting of the Holy Spirit was just so strong, I knew I would regret not heeding the call. So, I broke the silence by saying, "If there's nothing more to say, I think it's now my turn to lead everyone in prayer." I gathered my emotions and fought back my tears. If I was going to glorify God, I wanted to make sure everyone in the room understood me. I began by praising God for the gift of life; Ryan was still alive at the time. I thanked God for the gift of time; we still had time to be with Ryan. And there was still time to witness a miracle. I thanked God for every doctor in the room, for their love for Ryan, and for the truth that He loved him most. I prayed ever slowly and tried so hard to finish each sentence, pausing occasionally as I held back my tears. It was only through the Holy Spirit that I was able to pray what I prayed.

Later, Kaye told me they (Naty, Liezl, Cris, and herself) tried so hard not to cry while I was praying, but they still did. They wanted to get the lump out of their throats by crying out loud. I'm just grateful they didn't steal the scene. Seriously, I had no time to dwell on whatever emotion was running through my mind. I was devastated, to put it mildly. I was scared, but I continued to fix my eyes on God.

After praying, the doctors took turns shaking my hands and giving me words of encouragement, with some expressing admiration for my strength. If only they knew I was fighting so hard not to break inside; it wasn't the time to give up, not yet. Not yet, Lord...

After everyone left the conference room, I stayed behind and went over to Dr. Sadili who was seated across from me. I held her hand as she held mine.

"I fought so hard Marshi, only to be in this situation." ·

She was crying, and I was so touched by her love for Ryan and the family.

"I want to thank you for everything you've done, Doc. Nothing is impossible with God if He wills it."

Later, Kaye commented that I should be the one comforted by others. But in that instance, I was the one offering comfort to Dr. Sadili. True. God comforts us so we can comfort others.

We all went to see Ryan in the next room. I asked him, "Are you still fighting, Dad? Because I am..."

We sang the song "10,000 Reasons," because we had a thousand reasons to bless His Name, despite Ryan being medically brain dead. We cried so hard while we were inside Ryan's room.

Before Ryan got sick, I had been training for a 16 km run scheduled on September 22 in Amsterdam. Little did I know God registered me in a marathon.

It had been exactly three weeks since Ryan's admission to the hospital. It had been a journey!

From day one, we had prayed for Ryan to live and be healthy. Each day we saw miracles unfold one after another. From Ryan's medical condition to friends, family, and strangers growing in their spiritual walk, miracles happened every day these past weeks. Family, friends, doctors, and the entire medical team saw God's hand in this difficult time. This had been a test of faith, day in and day out.

On this day we were pushed to the limit. An EEG was scheduled to confirm whether Ryan was clinically brain dead. The doctors were just waiting for Ryan to be weaned off from the ECMO machine, which could happen on that day or the following day.

We cried. We had come so far only to be in this situation. After we cried, we continued to ask for the very same thing we'd been asking from day one — we asked God to let Ryan live and be healthy. We asked for a miracle the previous days; we continued to ask for a miracle that day.

This was not the time to give up. This was the time for us to depend more on God. We were at the point where science says Ryan's condition was irreversible. We only have God — the God who created all things; the God who sent His Son to die for our sins; the God who carried Ryan in His hands; the God who loved Ryan the most.

I looked at Ryan again before leaving the ICU. I whispered, "I love you."

Pinky went home to Taytay to be with Mama Nila. She told Mama Nila that Ryan's lungs, heart, and liver were healing but his brain was silent and that he was in a coma. She told Mama she felt the doctors were discouraged, even doubting. Mama told Pinky that God would give Ryan a new brain. He was fixing his brain because He would use Ryan for the ministry. Oh, the faith of a mother!

That night I hugged the kids.

I led the medical team in prayer at the conclusion
of what was to be the last family conference.

My moment with Dr. Sadili to thank her for
everything she has done for Ryan and the family.

The Calm Before the Storm

I went to Makati Med before lunch. It was still quiet. No visitors had arrived yet. I stood outside Ryan's window for an hour. I felt cold as I stood there, but it was okay. I felt so close to him that time as I quietly talked to him about us, the kids, and the future. I also talked to God. I told God, "Lord, now more than ever is the best time for you to wake Ryan up. It would be a miracle, and all glory will be to your Name alone! Imagine what a display of Your power that would be!" I was genuinely hopeful. Miracles do happen every day. My heart was at peace as I continued to hope.

I felt a gentle touch on my shoulder. One of Ryan's doctors was passing by and she stopped to talk to me. "Why don't you go inside and talk to him," she asked. "I'll just stay here, Doc," I said with a little smile. "How are you?" she continued to ask. I opened my mouth to answer, but then closed it again, afraid that my voice would tremble. With teary eyes I smiled at her. She understood and nodded. After patting my back, she left me alone.

Dr. Sadili visited Ryan. She said that the ECMO machine sweep was now at .5. That meant Ryan was able to excrete the carbon dioxide on his own. The RPM was down to 2750, from 3500. The only thing that was delaying Ryan's weaning off from the ECMO machine was the water in his lungs, but that would be addressed by the dialysis. All other numbers were stable. So, she said it was a good morning for her. That made me really smile this time. We were all just waiting for that miracle in the brain.

After standing for hours, I sat on our favorite seat in the ICU. For the past three weeks God preserved my health, until today. I started to feel feverish and cough. I decided to go home early and leave Ryan with our friends and family who had come to visit him. Before leaving the ICU, I got a call from our Dutch insurance company.

I have reproduced below my post on The Incredible Ryan page from September 5, 2019:

*****

We of little faith!

The Dutch insurance company called yesterday to inform me that they have made a one-time exception in Ryan's case. Normally, they would only cover the cost that was incurred if this happened in the Netherlands; however, in Ryan's case, they will cover 100% of the total bill as of yesterday, which stands at 8.7M pesos. They will need the latest prognosis to determine if they will still cover more in the coming days. Given Ryan's condition, they informed me that in the Netherlands, there is an option to pull the plug. I told them that we believe he will wake up and that we are not giving up. Of course, we cannot impose our faith. But as it is, 8.7M pesos is already a huge help!!! Thank you, Lord!!! Assuming the total bill will not exceed the original estimation of 15M pesos, we need to raise 6.3M pesos, of which we now have 3.1M pesos. God is amazing and thank you all for the love and support you've been giving the family. God will bless you more!

*****

"For my thoughts are not your thoughts, neither are your ways my ways," declares the LORD. "As the heavens are higher than the earth, so are my ways higher than your ways and my thoughts than your thoughts." (Isaiah 55:8-9 NIV)

It's a good reminder that we cannot limit God by our standards. We can trust God both in His unlimited power and His love for us.

At 8:00 a.m., Liezl was already at the Makati Med ICU. About an hour later, the window blind in Ryan's room was rolled up. Ryan was still on ECMO treatment. Kaye joined Liezl at Makati Med shortly thereafter. Dr. Sadili saw Ryan before lunchtime. On her way out of the ICU, Liezl and Kaye approached her to ask for updates. She told them she would like to talk to me at 3:00 p.m. and give her updates during the meeting. Family and friends started to arrive. Ryan received beautiful flowers from friends.

I just stayed at home in the morning because I was running a fever. The past weeks had now taken their toll on my health. I knew my health wasn't 100%. Even when I wasn't at Makati Med (that day and in the past weeks), I was always updated by family and friends who were manning the ICU. They would send me messages and pictures of almost everyone who had visited.

When I learned Dr. Sadili wanted to meet with me to give an update, I initially thought of skipping it and just asking my family to represent me. My family convinced me to go to Makati Med so I could also have myself checked by Dr. Sadili. So, at 3:00 p.m., I, together with Naty, Pinky, Kaye, Charo, and Cris, went to see Dr. Sadili in her clinic. It was a "standing room only" meeting and I was grateful that Dr. Sadili allowed everyone to attend.

Dr. Sadili was candid. She described Ryan like a car that had many broken parts. She had one question for me. She asked me where I stood now that we knew the condition of Ryan's brain. I told her to continue fighting and hope for a miracle, which could happen. I told her to tell the medical team not to give up yet, so that we were all aligned. She was happy to hear a definitive answer and assured us she would relay it to the doctors.

She then checked me, listened to my lungs and told me I had bronchitis. She prescribed my medicines and told me to stay at home for seven days to rest. She didn't want me to come to the hospital during that time; otherwise, she would make me sleep for days. We all left Makati Med after that. Cris and Pinky stayed behind; it was their turn to be the watchers until midnight. After midnight, Jen would relieve them.

We were required to have at least one watcher the entire time Ryan was in the ICU. The watcher or watchers would be the ones to sign off on all the requests of the doctors and nurses, and give urgent updates. There was never a time the ICU was unmanned. Relatives and friends who volunteered gave so much of their time and love for Ryan, for me. God never left our side. The outpouring of God's love is indescribable.

When we got home, I settled in bed, hoping to get the much-needed rest. I had less than two hours of peaceful time in my room, when our phones started beeping.

*****

Cris texted our "Titas of Manila" Viber group to give updates. Around 7:30 p.m., the neurologist seemed to have mistaken Cris for me and told Cris that Ryan was not looking good. His pupils were fixed dilated and there was no reaction from the brain stem. It was the medicines that were supporting Ryan. The neurologist said Ryan was having arrhythmia (i.e., his heart was having irregular rhythm). In short, Ryan's body was giving up. The doctor just wanted to let Cris (i.e., me) know; she knew the family had a strong faith. Cris thanked the doctor and told her the family would continue to pray for all the doctors. Meanwhile, Pinky was inside the ICU talking with Dr. Castro, the cardiologist from the ECMO team. We continued exchanging messages in our Viber group.

At 8:30, Cris updated us that Ryan was given medicine to increase his blood pressure. At the time, it was only 83/50.

Around 9:45, Cris told us that they had been asked to go inside the ICU so the doctors could update her and Pinky.

*****

At 9:51, Cris sent this message, "I think everybody should come here."

I was lying in bed when I saw the message. I still had a fever. Naty came into the room where Kaye and I were staying. She asked what time we would be ready. I told them I wasn't coming. Naty was surprised.

"Are you sure you're not coming?" she asked.

"I feel cold. It will be so cold there," I replied.

She looked at Kaye, then at me again.

"What if something happens tonight?" Naty asked.

I calmly said, "Nothing's going to happen tonight. Ryan will be ok."

I couldn't remember what I was thinking at the time. All I knew was I had faith Ryan wasn't going to die that day. Kaye left the room and went to Naty's room. When Kaye came back, she asked me again to join them. As a compromise, she said I could stay in the car in the basement parking of the hospital. I reluctantly agreed. I said bye to the kids and told them to pray for their dad.

On the way to Makati Med, we prayed for God to show us the power of His resurrection.

I knew Naty to be a fast driver. At the time, she must have gone beyond the speed limit on Skyway. We arrived at Makati Med in no time. I stayed in the car and slept, while Kaye and Naty went up to the ICU.

The other "Titas" arrived one by one — Liezl, Charo, Chilet, and her husband Bambi. They waited at the visitors' area outside the ICU, waiting for the doctors to talk to them.

At around 11:30, Kaye went down to the basement parking to check on me. I had slept in the car and felt better after having perspired there. We went to McDonalds just outside Makati Med to buy hot chocolate. Our order had not even arrived when Naty texted us that I was needed there. Kaye and I hurried to return to the ICU.

We all gathered in the visitors' area outside the ICU. Dr. Castro asked me again (they had asked me this question a few days ago), "Should Ryan arrest, should we resuscitate?"

I looked at Naty, as if to ask her.

"Marshi, 'wag na. Kawawa lang ang katawan ni Ryan." ("Marshi, not anymore. Ryan's body has had too much to bear already.")

I was silent for a while. I looked at each one of them. I knew they were all waiting for my answer. With a peaceful heart I said, "Ok, Doc, we won't try to revive him should he arrest. If it's God's will that Ryan lives, He will preserve his life."

Dr. Castro told me I needed to sign the DNR (Do not Resuscitate) waiver. But Dr. Sadili said, "Please, let's not subject Marshi to that anymore. Let her sister, Doc Naty, sign it."

Dr. Sadili held my hand, and, together, we walked inside the ICU towards Ryan's room. Everyone followed.

At midnight, I was outside Ryan's room with Naty, Pinky, Kaye, Cris, Liezl, Charo, and Chilet. Bambi stayed outside the ICU and waited at the visitors' area.

Dr. Castro explained to us that they had given all the medicines to Ryan to keep his heart from failing. He asked us if we still wanted to continue so they could order again for the day. It was so difficult to think and decide. It was like his destiny was put in my hands. I cannot remember how I answered this question.

I wouldn't describe the situation as frantic. The doctors and nurses moved calmly, checking on Ryan's vital signs and the monitors every few moments. All of us were sitting, praying, or talking quietly in the ICU just outside Ryan's room.

One of the doctors asked us if we wanted to talk to Ryan. The doctor said that hearing is thought to be the last sense to go. Pinky and Kaye each talked to Ryan. Then Naty asked me, "Shouldn't Sam be here now?"

I wasn't sure I wanted Sam to be there. Having Sam come to the hospital at that time meant Ryan was about to die. What happened to believing that a miracle would happen? But looking at Ryan and with his vital signs going down, I had to admit that it was just a matter of time.

I couldn't decide. We all discussed it and exchanged opinions. One of the Titas said I had to give Sam a chance to decide if she wanted to see her dad before he died, because she might later resent that I had denied her the opportunity.

I asked to speak to Ryan. I put on a gown, head cap, and gloves and went to Ryan's bedside. "Are you going already, Dad? Are you tired of fighting? Do you want me to stop fighting?" I cried as I asked God if it was time already.

I rejoined the group and agreed for Sam to be brought to the hospital so she could see her dad one last time. Kaye and Cris went to get her.

At 12:54, my sister Ann sent this message to the group, "Praying the Holy Spirit teaches us all how to pray." When I read this message, I fully surrendered to His will. He gives life, He takes it away. Blessed be His name at all times.

We all waited for Sam to arrive. It seemed like a long time, but Cris and Kaye had just been away for a few minutes. Naty texted Kaye and Cris to hurry up. I learned later on they had difficulty waking Sam up. Sam must have felt disoriented that at 1:00 a.m., Tita Cris and Tita Kaye were waking her up, telling her that mommy wanted to see her at the hospital.

At 1:25, Sam arrived at the ICU. I met her in the hallway before she reached her dad's room. I hugged her long and tight. Then we stood at the door of Ryan's room. I explained to her that dad wouldn't wake up. The doctors said that his heart was already weak and his body was giving up.

"Sam, Dad might go to heaven soon. Remember, we talked about this already? God gave us life. He can take it away, too."

She was very quiet. We sat down outside Ryan's room but Sam felt cold. We went outside of the ICU and sat in the waiting area.

At 2:20, Sam and I were asked to go back inside the ICU. We were told the time might come any minute now. We all gathered around Ryan. I stood beside him and leaned toward him, my hand on his chest. I wanted to hug him and never let go.

It was a scene that you'd see only in movies. We all knew it was only a matter of time, but by God's grace, Sam and I and everyone else were calm, some quietly shedding tears.

Pinky led us in singing the hymn "Great is Thy Faithfulness." Indeed, every day we saw new mercies. God carried us through the past twenty-four days.

We next sang "It Is Well With My Soul." This hymn was written by Horatio Spafford after he lost his four daughters in a sea tragedy. Despite his grief, he chose to praise God for His goodness and His great love for us by dying on the cross for the forgiveness of our sins. A portion of the beautiful lyrics reads:

When peace like a river, attendeth my way,
When sorrows like sea billows roll
Whatever my lot, thou hast taught me to say
It is well, it is well, with my soul
It is well with my soul
It is well, it is well with my soul
Though Satan should buffet, though trials should come,
Let this blest assurance control,
That Christ has regarded my helpless estate,
And hath shed His own blood for my soul
It is well with my soul
It is well, it is well with my soul
My sin, oh, the bliss of this glorious thought
My sin, not in part but the whole,
Is nailed to the cross, and I bear it no more,

Praise the Lord, praise the Lord, O my soul . . .

"Whatever my lot, thou hast taught me to say, It is well with my soul." Whatever God wills in my life, in Ryan's life, I accept. The Lord gave, and the Lord has taken away. To love God is to accept His will in our lives.

By the time we got to the third stanza, I was already crying so hard. And for the first time since Ryan got sick, I heard Sam crying out loud behind me and turned to see Naty hugging her. I went to her and hugged her while we both cried.

She asked, "Why?" I replied, "I don't know. I also asked why, and I don't know the answer. What I know is that God is good." She looked at me and nodded her head. Sam also believed in the goodness and love of God. It was easy for her to accept that even when we don't understand, we can rest in the truth that God is good.

I went back to Ryan's side and we sang "10,000 Reasons," a song that will always remind me of Ryan, a song that Shaun still loves to sing.

Pinky said a brief prayer for Ryan. It was 2:40 when we finished singing and praising God for Ryan's life.

I finally said goodbye to Ryan. I thanked him for fighting a good fight. I told him we would miss him so much. And that I loved him.

The doctors checked on him. I hugged Sam as we looked at the monitors and waited until the line went flat and the numbers reached zero. I was blessed the doctors allowed all of us inside

Ryan's room to be with him. Dr. Sadili hugged me, then Sam, and said she was sorry she wasn't able to help her dad.

At 2:45, Ryan finally went home to heaven. I looked at him, smiled and told him to enjoy heaven.

PART IV

AND HE CARRIES ME THROUGH

I woke up at 7:00 a.m., and because of habit, I sat down and began to pray. "Good morning Lord, thank you for this day, for the gift of life. Dear God, I pray for Ryan, please . . ." and then I stopped. It dawned on me Ryan had died already. The twenty-five-day journey had ended.

I checked my phone and was surprised that many had sent messages of comfort and love for us even though I had not informed them of Ryan's death. I wasn't upset. I was just surprised how fast the word spread.

Before Pinky and I parted ways in the hospital that early morning, we agreed not to tell their relatives yet until she had the chance to tell Mama.

I posted on the Facebook page that our Incredible Ryan had gone to be with the Lord at 2:45 a.m. He had fought a good fight, and I was so proud of him. I ended it with Philippians 1:21 (NIV): "For to me, to live is Christ and to die is gain."

I wasn't prepared for this day. I couldn't bear to think of how the kids would feel, especially Sam. A close friend in Amsterdam texted Sam and asked how she was. Sam replied, "Happy and sad. Happy because Dad is now in heaven."

What a gift it was to know Ryan is home with the Lord. It made the reality of death more acceptable, letting go of a loved one less difficult, and the grieving more bearable.

The Lord blessed me tremendously that day. His love for us flowed through the family and friends who were there for us, who helped in so many different ways. Kaye and Pinky waited in the hospital until early morning to complete Ryan's final details, then drove to Taytay so Pinky could deliver the news to Mama Nila. Charo and Naty took care of the arrangements for the cremation, wake, and inurnment. Cristy and Jen came to the house to get photos for the video presentation to be shown at the wake. Danielle took care of reproducing enlarged photos of Ryan for the wake. She also bought white tops for the kids and me to be used during the two-day wake and inurnment. Bing and Neneng, dear family and friends, came to the house to spend time with the kids.

Later in the day, Kaye and Cris went back to Makati Med to settle the outstanding hospital and doctors' bill. A death certificate was needed for the cremation, and it would only be issued by the hospital if we had fully settled the medical expenses. The billing department informed them that the doctors' fees totaled two million four hundred thousand pesos, which we had to pay in cash on that day so the cremation could proceed as scheduled.

The total hospital bill was more than twelve million pesos. Eight million seven hundred thousand pesos of the total bill was already guaranteed by the Dutch insurance company and we had made initial payments amounting to two million two hundred thousand pesos in the first week of Ryan's admission at Makati Med. We thought we only had to raise the remaining one million one hundred thousand pesos to complete the total bill. Makati Med, however, required the entire two million four hundred thousand pesos in doctors' fees be paid in cash.

The Lord knew I didn't have that money. He used family and friends who generously and without hesitation almost emptied their bank accounts that day. It was God's miracle that we were able to complete the amount needed in so short a time. After Kaye and Cris completed their banking transactions, they returned to Makati Med.

It was already 5:00 p.m., and Kaye and Cris were still at the billing department. I texted and asked what was taking them so long and if something was wrong. They responded that the Dutch insurance company had asked them to wait because they were finalizing the amount they would cover and coordinating it with their local counterpart. It was both a test of patience with the process and trust that there was a reason for the long wait.

Finally, they were informed that the total bill of more than twelve million pesos would be covered in full by the Dutch insurance company! We were in awe, totally in awe! From the beginning, we knew that if God allowed this to happen, He would provide for our needs because He is faithful. God honored our faith in Him.

Because I did not need to shell out money for the doctors' fees, I returned the two million four hundred thousand pesos to those who had loaned their savings to me.

We had raised a total of three million one hundred thousand pesos through GoGetFunding, both online and offline. I returned most of the amounts that were donated through the crowdfunding and retained a small amount for the wake and inurnment expenses.

The Lord was amazingly gracious! Things would have been so different if I ended up with a huge debt after losing Ryan. I cried to the Lord rejoicing because He remained faithful in providing for our financial needs. He sent people to help me take care of everything that needed to be done that day.

There was much crying that day, but there was also a lot of rejoicing. My heart was at peace. And my physical body rested.

POSTSCRIPT

September 6, 2020

Shaun woke up from a restful night.

"Good morning, Shaun!" I greeted him. "Do you know what day it is today?"

Shaun, as he was trying to open his eyes, slowly shook his head.

"Today is Dad's first year anniversary in heaven!" I exclaimed with much enthusiasm. The thing is, I wasn't sure myself how I would be feeling today. But for the kids' sake, I wanted to create an atmosphere of celebration, celebrating the perfect life Ryan is now enjoying in heaven.

"Are we going there, Mommy?"

"Not today Shaun, we are not going to heaven today."

I carried Shaun in my arms and we went down to the kitchen.

Two days ago, I had a beautiful conversation with Sam about this day. I asked her if she knew what made September 6 special. She said it marked the first year since her dad had gone home to heaven. After Ryan died, and even up to this time, Sam's outlook has not changed; she misses her dad but doesn't want to be sad, so she thinks only about the happy memories we had as a family.

It has been a year of God's faithfulness. From the day Ryan fell ill, to the day God took him home, and up to this very day, God has been my constant rock. He has sustained me. He has never failed me and the kids, not even once!

I still don't have the answer to Sam's question during Ryan's dying moments. I may never know the answer in this lifetime; but looking back, I see God's sovereignty. He orchestrated everything for the completion of His good and perfect plan.

You see, I always say, "If God wants to really bless you with the best job ever, He can create a company just so you can have that job." I guess that happened to me in 2014 when I was offered the chief financial officer position at the subsidiary of a Dutch bank in Manila. The subsidiary was set up in mid-2013, and they decided to hire their first CFO following their first year of operation. After three years into the role, and after the birth of another child, I was offered a position at the Head Office in the Netherlands.

After seeking God's direction for our family, we migrated to Europe in the spring of 2018. God had been so good to our family. Our time in the Netherlands was the best part of our family life. After fifteen months, we returned to the Philippines for a vacation. And that's when things took a different course.

Since the beginning of time, God had written Ryan's life story to be completed in forty years. By God's providence, all that had happened was according to his plan. Psalm 139:16 (NIV) says ". . . all the days ordained for me were written in your book before one of them came to be." I thank God for making sure we were in the Philippines when Ryan died. Why did God give me a job at this Dutch company? Why did He have to bring us to the Netherlands for such a short time as fifteen months? Because He wanted to use the Dutch insurance company to provide for the financial needs of the family. Because He wanted the family to enjoy the simple life in the Netherlands, embrace the cool weather we all loved, and cherish the quiet and loving moments we had as a family. As God knew that it was going to be Ryan's last year with us, He allowed us to create the best memories, both as husband and wife and as a family. Without any doubt, it was a great display of His sovereignty over our lives.

Early this year 2020, many have asked, "Wasn't it COVID-19?" It seemed like it, but we can only speculate. There is no way to confirm this anymore. But yes, it could have been COVID-19. Ryan could have been patient number one in the Philippines. What I am certain of is God walked beside me during that time of Ryan's sickness. God is walking beside me now. And I can rest in the truth that God will walk beside me until I finish my own race.

Now the family is back in Manila. I am confident this is where God intends us to be in this season of our lives. Even as the world seems to pause for a moment during this pandemic, I see God's goodness and faithfulness moment by moment. I know that whatever life brings, wherever life takes us, Christ is enough for us.

"Heavenly Father, will you please whisper to Ryan we miss him so much down here?"

Love,
Marshi, Sam, and Shaun

ACKNOWLEDGMENTS

I have reserved this space for the two beautiful people God has given me as I wrote this book.

In three different countries with two time zones, our small team of three enjoyed what has become a journey in itself as we wrote and rewrote the lines of this story.

To Kaye, who walked with us during The Incredible Ryan journey, thank you for recounting those twenty-five days with me one day at a time, a year later. You loved Ryan as a brother in the Lord, and you have become the fifth member of the Brozo family. I know you grieve as much as I do with his loss. As we worked on this book, I hope that it has helped you heal, as it has helped me. I cannot thank you enough for all the hours you've put into this book, day and night. This book would not be as beautiful as it is now without your invaluable inputs. But most of all, I cannot thank you enough for all the love you have for the kids and me. You are a precious gift to us!

To my Tita Laurie, we met only two weeks ago. I am thankful to the Lord for causing our paths to cross at this point in my journey. As a stranger, you read the draft of this book, chewed on every word that was written, provided language comments and grammar edits, and shared your personal insights as you went through each of the twenty-five days. Your insights have been a tremendous encouragement to me and a confirmation from God that He wanted His story to be written in this book for His glory. Now, not only do I have this book, but I also gained a beautiful friendship with a treasured friend across the globe. What have I done to deserve you? I will pray for that day to come when I can meet you in person and, perhaps, enjoy your banana muffins and sit in your rocking chair.

God, in His infinite wisdom, uses ordinary people to accomplish extraordinary things. Kaye and Tita Laurie, we are just ordinary people. But when we make ourselves available, He can accomplish great and mighty things through us, for His glory.

Thank you for sharing your lives with me. I am forever grateful.

Marshi
Manila, September 2020

ABOUT THE AUTHOR

 Maricor, or Marshi to family and friends, is an accountant by profession. She grew up and studied in Leyte, Philippines. She considers her faith and family to be most important to her. A friend once joked that if she joined a beauty pageant, she would win the Miss Congeniality award hands down. She finds joy in meeting new people and developing beautiful friendships. If she isn't spending time with her family, she keeps herself busy in the kitchen preparing food for her kids. She loves Hawaiian pizza, which some say is not a real pizza.

Maricor and her family lived in Amsterdam between 2018 and 2019, and are presently residing in Metro Manila, Philippines. *Walking Beside Me* is her first book.

In memory of our Incredible Ryan

July 2018, First summer in Amsterdam

Dec 2018, Christmas in London

January 2019, First family winter with snowman

March 2019, 11th wedding anniversary
celebration in Pilatus, Switzerland

Printed in Great Britain
by Amazon